Calvary Cemetery
Old and New Sections

Cemetery Inscriptions

Washington Township, Clermont County, Ohio

Compiled by:
Pamela Kellum Smith
Clermont County Genealogical Society

1600
Alphabetical
Inscriptions

Old and New Calvary Cemetery

St. Rt. 756, Washington Township
GPS   N38° 52.170   W084° 10.202, Elev. 780, within 21 ft.

Take St. Rt. 52 from Cincinnati, pass through New Richmond. At Point
Pleasant make a left on St. Rt. 232, make a right onto St. Rt. 756. Pass
Washington Township Park. Cross St. Rt. 743. Old Cemetery located on
right across from church and New Calvary Cemetery located by the church.
Park at church. Easy Access.

I have been working on this cemetery off and on for the past eight years.
Each time I visited I always found something new or a correction.   Please
understand some of the stones were impossible for me to read, so I did my
best to interpret.

Stones we could not locate previously recorded:

Inez E. Brown
Mary E. Blackburn
GEN Fee
John Eskam
Clayton Camery
PHI Camery
A.M. Camerer
M. Boys
Jonathan Boys
Edith Brown
Jane McKinley
Joseph McWilliams
George F. Norris
Ida May Amsbury
Emma F. Blackburn
R. Jones
Bart Lough
George Manning
Leeana Rush
Mary Sapp

Old Calvary Cemetery

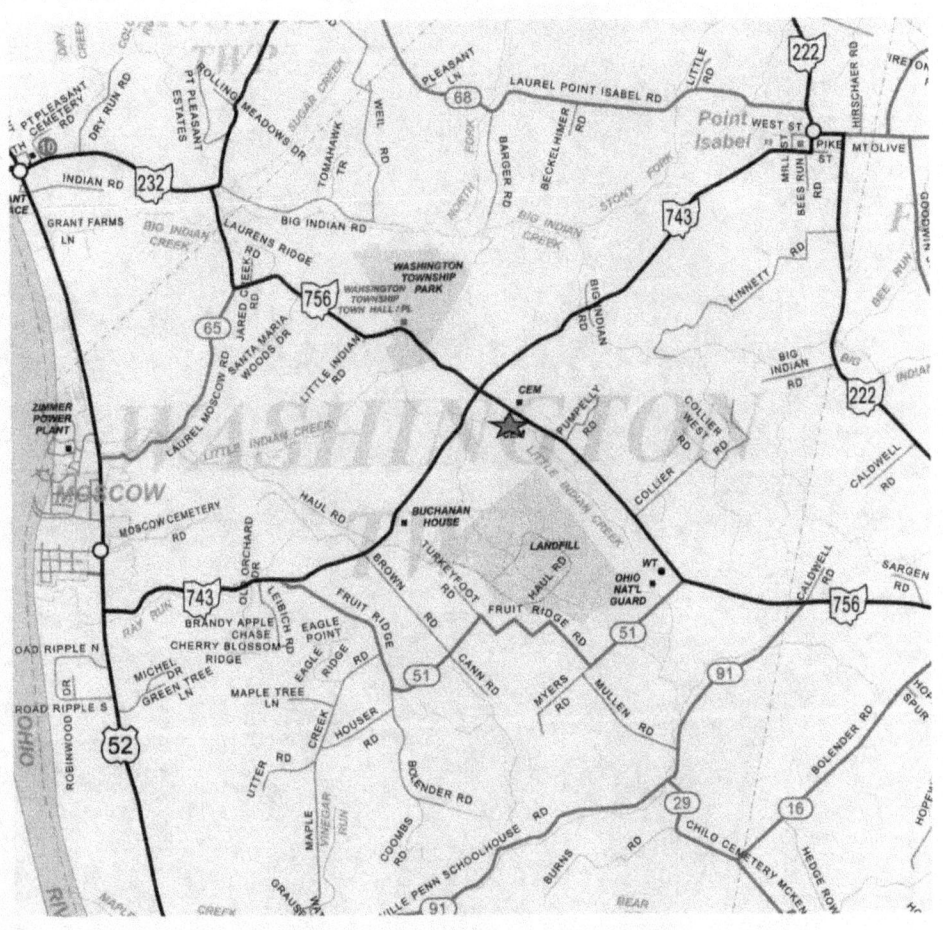

Calvary Cemetery
Pam's assigned sections

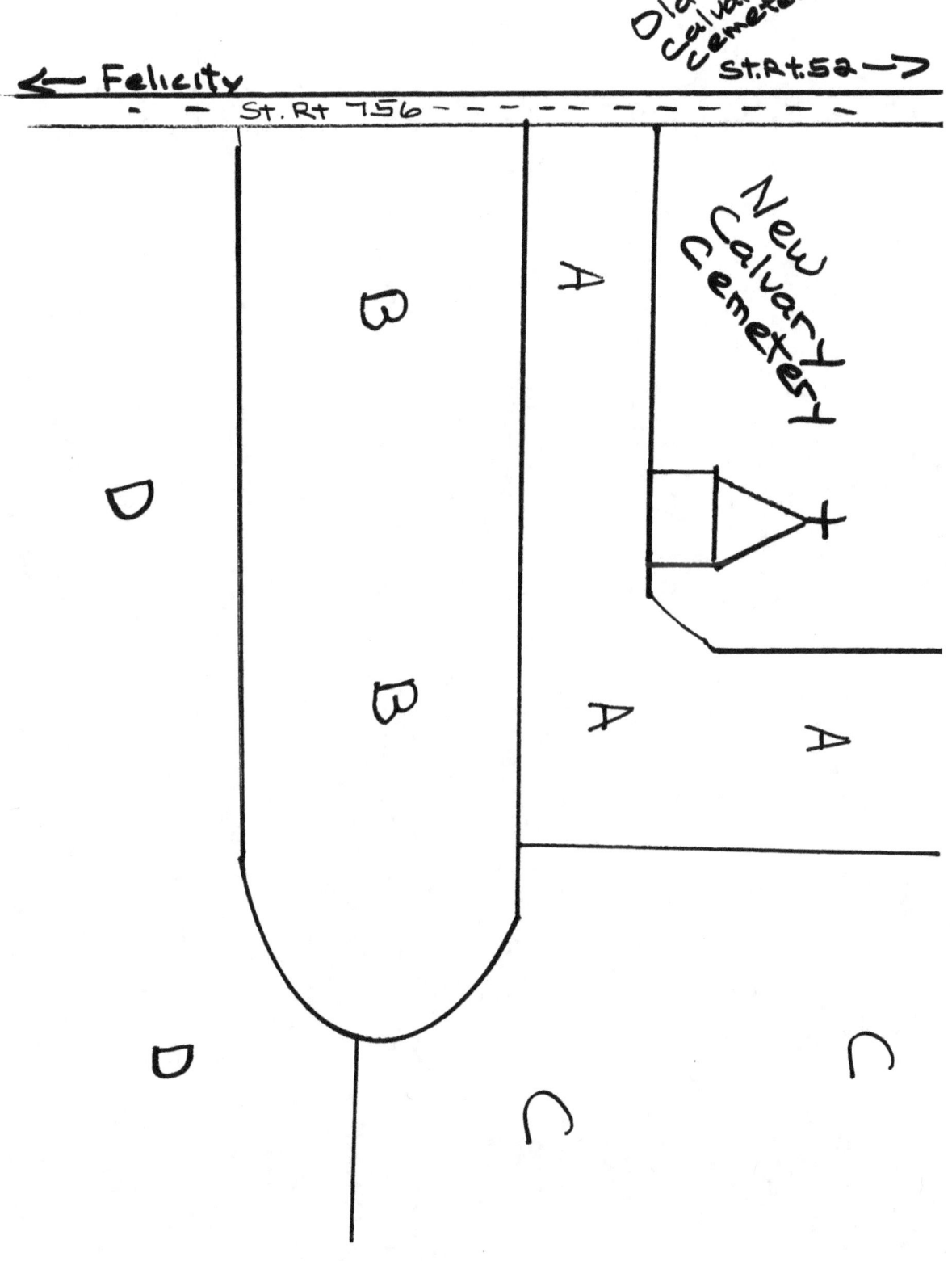

Calvary Cemetery Old and New Sections

Abraham	Emeline T.	wife of James W. Abraham, born Nov 25, 1830, died Dec 16, 1894	Old Section
Abraham	Emerson R.	born Feb 17, 1857, died Aug 7, 1858	Old Section
Abraham	Enoch	died Jan 20, 1865, aged 33 years	Old Section
Abraham	Frank A.	died Oct 23, 1865, aged 8y 25d, child of E & SJ Abraham	Old Section
Abraham	Hattie R.	born Nov 27, 1850, died Aug 25, 1865	Old Section
Abraham	J. Markley	died Mar 24, 1864, aged 1y 2m 6d, child of E & SJ Abraham	Old Section
Abraham	James W.	born Sep 18, 1824, died Nov 7, 1875	Old Section
Abraham	Lemuel	born 1828, died 1868	Old Section
Abraham	Myrtle C.	born Feb 22, 1870, died Jul 7, 1871, child of W & ET Abraham	Old Section
Abraham	Willie C.	born Mar 1, 1863, died Sep 5, 1865, child of W & ET Abraham	Old Section
Abrams	Charlotte	died 1898	Sect B
Abrams	Corrine McCullough	dau of J & E McCullough, 1917	Sect D
Abrams	Edwin A.	1859-1908	Sect B
Abrams	Eliza J.	1834-1915	Sect B
Abrams	Infant Son	Apr 30, 1897 son of WJ & Maggie Abrams	Sect D
Abrams	J. H.	monument	Sect B
Abrams	Jennie B.	wife of Edwin A. Abrams, 1859-1942	Sect B
Abrams	Jessie	1869-1954	Sect B
Abrams	John H.	1855-1919	Sect B
Abrams	Justis	died 1896	Sect B
Abrams	Maggie	1860-1932	Sect D
Abrams	Markley, J.	1867-1906	Sect D
Abrams	Marshall	May 30, 1887 - Jan 31, 1956	Sect D
Abrams	Ray W.	Dec 24, 1931 - Nov 23, 1932	Sect D
Abrams	Sadie E. Schwab	Jul 27, 1893 - Nov 6, 1993	Sect D
Abrams	Walter	1859-1946	Sect D
Abrams	William	born Sep 12, 1826 , died Sep 8, 1904	Sect B
Ackley	James, Corporal	Co E 175 Ohio Inf.	Sect B
Ackley	Mary J.	wife of James Ackley, 1827-1896	Sect B
Adrian	Albert	CPL US Army, WWI, 1886-1980	Sect A
Adrian	Anna	born Schmidt, Gott in Von, wife of Wilhelm F.D. Adrian, born May 24, 1815, died Aug 20, 1877	Old Section
Adrian	Carrie	born Oct 22, 1850 - Blank	Sect B
Adrian	Catharina	dau of Joh. & Margaretha Adrian, born May 20, 1878, died Jun 18, 1878	Old Section
Adrian	Celia J.	1892-1955	Sect A
Adrian	Edward	1891-1892	Sect B
Adrian	Irene M.	1904-1988	Sect A
Adrian	John G.	1884-1966	Sect A
Adrian	Maria	born Adrian, Gath Von Konig, Kirk, born Aug 28, 1854, died Jan 1, 1886	Old Section

Calvary Cemetery Old and New Sections

Surname	Given Name	Details	Section
Adrian	Wilhelm F. D.	born March 16, 1814, died Dec 22, 1879	Old Section
Adrian	William	Jan 9, 1843 - Jan 6, 1903	Sect B
Airey	Anna M.	1860-1936	Old Section
Aites	William E.	US Army Feb 5, 1938 - Jul 25, 2002	Sect C
Albrecht	Mary Ann Boots	Aug 8, 1936 - Apr 2, 1999	Sect C
Altman	Charles S.	1890-1911	Sect D
Altman	Clarence	1879-grown in tree. (born Nov 14, 1879, died Feb 25, 1915, son of Phillip and Mary Altman)	Sect D
Altman	Harry P.	1883-1908	Sect D
Altman	Mary C.	wife of Philip D. Altman, 1850-1927	Sect D
Altman	Philip D.	1842-1915	Sect D
Altman	Ruth	Infant daughter of DT & M Altman	Sect D
Amsbury	Ida May	dau of William H. & M. Amsbury, died Jan 10, 1864, aged 3y 5m 18d (STONE MISSING)	Old Section
Anter	Joann Croswell	Feb 2, 1940 - Jun 23, 2001	Sect D
Armacost	Delila	wife of Levi Armacost, born Mar 10, 1799, died May 4, 1820, 21y 1m 24ds	Old Section
Ashley	Almina G.	1843-1886	Sect B
Augst	Mcheala K.	Jul 25, 1996 - Jan 30, 2000	Sect B
Augst	Micheal, Jr.	Jan 7, 1998 - Jan 30, 2000	Sect B
B	N.	Marker	Sect A
Baird	Naomi Wethington	Jun 21, 1926 - Mar 14, 2001	Sect D
Baker	Lester	Mar 8, 1932 - Jul 23, 1998, Korean Veteran	Sect C
Baker	Lester Lee	US Army Korea, Mar 8, 1932 - Jul 23, 1998	Sect C
Ballard	Effie	1890-1972	Sect D
Ballard	Huse	Ohio PVT US Army WWI, Oct 19, 1891 - Feb 17, 1970	Sect D
Ballentine	George Porter	born Jul 12, 1858 in West Virginia, died Jan 28, 1884, aged 25y 6m 15d	Old Section
Balog	Bernard A.	T SGT US Army WWII, May 25, 1913 - Jan 3, 2006	Sect D
Balog	Bernhard Alois	May 25, 1913 - Jan 3, 2006	Sect D
Balog	Rachel V. Benjamin Herbert	Aug 24, 1923 - Apr 18, 1990	Sect D
Banks	Burnest	PFC US Army WWII, May 29, 1918 - Mar 14, 1992	Sect A
Banks	Burnest	May 29, 1918 - Mar 14, 1992, wed Oct 21, 1941 to Irene King	Sect A
Banks	Connie M.	Nov 19, 1947 - Blank, wed Mar 31, 1966 to Phillip L. Banks	Sect D
Banks	Irene King	May 28, 1921 - Apr 16, 1990, wed Oct 21, 1941 to Burnest Banks	Sect A
Banks	Phillip L.	Jan 22, 1947 - May 11, 2011, wed Mar 31, 1966 to Connie M.	Sect D
Barber	Eliza Jane	dau of James and Margaret Barber, died Apr1 5, 1850 - aged 16y 4m 14d	Old Section
Barber	Margaret	wife of James Barber, born Feb 27, 1802, died Nov 24, 1844	Old Section
Barber	Mattie A. B.	dau of James and Margaret Barber, died Jan 16, 1867, aged 29y 11m 27d	Old Section
Barker	Sue Moreton	Mar 24, 1890- Jul 19, 1983	Sect B
Barkley	Bell R.	dau of Jos & F Barkley, died Jul 3, 1872, aged 21 years	Old Section

Calvary Cemetery Old and New Sections

Surname	First Name	Details	Section
Barkley	Florella	wife of Joseph Barkley, died Mar 18, 1871, aged 60 years	Old Section
Barkley	George	died Apr 21, 1837 in 71st year	Old Section
Barkley	John	died Feb 20, 1839 in 38th year	Old Section
Barkley	Joseph	died Dec 8, 1870, aged 67 years	Old Section
Barkley	Joseph H.	son of J & F Barkley, died Mar 17, 1871, aged 25 yrears	Old Section
Barkley	Lizzie S.	dau of J&F Barkley, died Dec 18, 1876 aged 29 years	Old Section
Barkley	Margaret	wife of John Barkley, born Dec 15, 1804, died Mar 2, 1881	Old Section
Barkley	Rebecca	wife of William Barkley, died Feb 25, 1864, aged 89y 2m 21ds	Old Section
Barkley	Sarah R.	dau of Joseph & Florella Barkley, died Jun 28, 1845 in 10th year	Old Section
Barkley	W. G.	born Jun 18, 1838, died Sep 27, 1879	Old Section
Barkley	William	died Sep 27, 1833, aged 63y 7m 6ds (2 stones)	Old Section
Bartley	James R.	son of William C. & Martha Bartley, died Jan 14, 1850, aged 2m 8ds	Old Section
Bauer	Carolyn J.	Apr 24, 1926 - Blank	Sect D
Bauer	Lee	1888-1978	Sect D
Bauer	Lester	Nov 29, 1923 - Sep 5, 1982	Sect D
Bauer	Lester W.	Tec 4 US Army, WWII, Nov 29, 1923 - Sep 5, 1982	Sect D
Bauer	Neva M.	1895-1943	Sect D
Beckelhimer	Elizabeth A.	1847-1904	Sect D
Beckelhimer	George	1838-1903	Sect D
Beckelhimer	Wilson	1883-1941	Sect D
Begley	Bert	CPL US Army, WWII, Feb 28, 1918 - Jun 10, 2002	Sect C
Begley	Bert	Feb 28, 1918 - Jun 10, 2002, wed Dec 20, 1949 to Malvery Roberts	Sect C
Begley	Malvery Roberts	Jan 13, 1928 - Blank, wed Dec 20, 1949 to Bert Begley	Sect C
Belt	Estel R.	Oct 20, 1911 - Aug 5, 1979	Sect D
Belt	Ruth A. Allen	Mar 24, 1915 - May 14, 1997	Sect D
Benjamin	A.	was born in the year of our Lord 1837 and died in 1851	Old Section
Benjamin	Bertha Louise Russell	May 14, 1930 - Mar 15, 2008. wed Nov 12, 1948 to Carl Dennis Benajmin	Sect C
Benjamin	Carl Dennis	May 13, 1929 - Blank, wed Nov 12, 1948 to Bertha Louise Russell	Sect C
Benjamin	Charles R.	SSGT US Army, WWII, Sep 1, 1922 - Jun 7, 1989	Sect C
Benjamin	Charles R.	Sep 1, 1922 - Jun 7, 1989	Sect C
Benjamin	Dora Blair	Jul 16, 1920 - Blank	Sect C
Benjamin	Fredrick	May 20, 1901 - Sep 24, 1994	Sect A
Benjamin	John L.	1876-1932	Sect D
Benjamin	Mary L.	1880-1950	Sect D
Benjamin	W.B.	born 4th Feb, 1856, died 7 Aug 1863 (handwritten)	Old Section
Bennett	Belle B.	1855-1916	Sect B
Bennett	Erma P.	1920-1970	Sect A
Bennett	Frank E.	Jun 15, 1912 - Mar 2, 1981	Sect A

Calvary Cemetery Old and New Sections

Last Name	First Name	Details	Section
Bennett	Frank E.	PVT US Army, WWII, Jun 15, 1912 - Mar 2, 1981	Sect A
Bennett	Fred W.	1914-1998	Sect A
Bennett	Garnet E.	1885-1929	Sect B
Bennett	George L.	1856-1940	Sect B
Bennett	Jesse B.	1895-1964	Sect B
Bennett	Sarah B. Benjamin Waters	Apr 5, 1912 - Dec 5, 1977	Sect A
Bennett	Victor A.	Sep 15, 1947 - Jan 7, 2004	Sect A
Bevis	James Dellano	Jun 15, 1945 - Oct 8, 1978	Sect C
Bieman	John L.	1896-1981	Sect D
Bieman	Minnie I.	1895-1981	Sect D
Blackburn	Caroline	dau of JW & S Blackburn, died Aug 17, 1843, aged 2y 3m 15ds	Old Section
Blackburn	Emma F.	died Sep 17 1839, aged 2y 24d, child of James K. & Susan A. Blackburn,(STONE MISSING)	Old Section
Blackburn	Mary E.	died Sep 18, 1860, aged 11y 3m 24d, child of James K & Susan A. Blackburn, (STONE MISSING)	Old Section
Blackburn	Richard Lee	Aug 17, 1980 - Sep 17, 1998	Sect D
Boggess	Rachael	born Jan 25, 1819, died Feb 1, 1895 (on David Brannen monument)	Old Section
Boggs	Bessie M.	Nov 8, 1929 - Aug 8, 1998	Sect C
Bolender	Hazel	1905-1995	Sect A
Bolender	Martha J.	1943-2007	Sect A
Bolender	Walter D.	1900-1968	Sect A
Boner	Ella D.	wife of GM Boner, died Oct 27, 1879, aged 27y 4m 21d	Old Section
Boner	Geo M.	Co F 89 Ohio Inf.	Old Section
Boots	Katherine Hull	wife of Charles Boots, Apr 2, 1917 - Aug 3, 1993	Sect C
Bosse	Archie	1914-1985	Sect D
Bosse	Helen	1914-1969	Sect D
Bowling	Dealie M.	Nov 5, 1941 - Blank	Sect C
Bowling	Donald R.	1969-2011	Sect C
Bowling	Joe	PVT US Army, May 21, 1938 - Nov 27, 2010	Sect C
Bowling	Joe, Sr.	May 21, 1938 - Nov 27, 2010	Sect C
Bowling	Pearl	Sep 30, 1914 - Jul 23, 1980	Sect C
Boys	Clarissa	died Aug 7, 1882, aged 66 years	Old Section
Boys	Delia A.	dau of James and Clarisa S, Boys, died Feb 6, 1866, aged 8ys 3m 16d	Old Section
Boys	James	died Nov 8, 1898, aged 88y 10m	Old Section
Boys	James A.	son of James and Clarisa S. Boys, died Aug 23, 1868, aged 23y 1m 27d	Old Section
Boys	Jonathan	husband of Amanda E. Boys, died Sep 24, 1853, aged 33y 26d (STONE MISSING)	Old Section
Boys	M	Dec-Jun 20, 1823 (STONE MISSING)	Old Section
Boys	Mary J.	dau of William& XXXXXX Boys, died Jan 11, 1850, aged 4m	Old Section
Boys	William H.	son of JF & E Boys, died Mar 14, 1864, aged 20y 11m 1d	Old Section

4

Calvary Cemetery Old and New Sections

Surname	Given	Details	Section
Brannen	David	died Apr 16, 1841, aged 58y 1m 9d	Old Section
Brannen	David M.	born Sep 23, 1820, died Feb 14, 1892, aged 71y 4m 21ds	Old Section
Brannen	H. E.	1843-1927	Old Section
Brannen	J. B.	1832-1891	Old Section
Brannen	Martha	wife of David Brannen, died Aug 30, 1858, aged 71y 13d	Old Section
Brannen	Martha Jane Wedding	born Dec 11, 1845, died Dec 4, 1931	Old Section
Brannon	David	died Apr 16, 1841, in 59th year	Old Section
Bravard	Arley E.	KY Stab Sgt 309 Engineer TN WW1, Oct 9, 1895 - Jun 12, 1954	Sect D
Bravard	Earl W.	PVT US Army, WWII, 1924-1975	Sect B
Brawley	John	1851-1932	Sect D
Brawley	Mary A.	1853-1899	Sect D
Brill	Chad Edward	Jan 26, 1981 - Jun 23, 2002	Sect D
Brondhaver	Etta F.	Nov 5, 1942 - Jan 9, 2002, wed Feb 10, 1972 to Leslie F.	Sect B
Brondhaver	Leslie F.	Oct 9, 1947 - Blank, wed Feb 10, 1972 to Etta F.	Sect B
Brooks	George E.	Jul 27, 1926 - Jul 4, 1998	Sect D
Brooks	Lula	Oct 28, 1923 - Apr 12, 2001	Sect D
Brown	David	son of John and Sarah Brown, died Aug 7, 1843, aged 3y 5m 27d	Old Section
Brown	Donald J.	Sep 11, 1935 - Jun 16, 2008	Sect A
Brown	Dwight	1885-1965	Sect B
Brown	Edith	dau of JR and SA Brown, died Jul 26, 1865, aged 26d (STONE MISSING)	Old Section
Brown	Emily F.	Jun 3, 1934 - Oct 13, 1996	Sect B
Brown	Inez E.	1863-1894 - dau of John R. & Sarah Brown (STONE MISSING)	Sect B
Brown	John	died Jun 12, 1851, aged 60 years	Old Section
Brown	John R.	1837-1922	Sect B
Brown	Lucetta	1827-1907	Sect B
Brown	Maggie	1837-1908	Sect D
Brown	Robert	died Nov 21, 1861 in his 89th year	Old Section
Brown	Ruth	consort of Robert Brown, died Oct 16, 1847, aged 70y 7m	Old Section
Brown	Sarah A.	1843-1904	Sect B
Brown	Sarah A.	wife of John Brown, died Feb 7, 1887 - 75 years (buried In Sabetha Cemetery, Nemana Co., Kansas)	Old Section
Buchanan	A.	died in 1803 (GAR) marker	Old Section
Buchanan	A.	footstone AB	Old Section
Buchanan	Alexander	Ohio Rev War	Old Section
Buchanan	America M.	dau of John G & Catharine M. Buchanan died Jan 13, 1834, aged 3y 2m 9d	Old Section
Buchanan	Andrew	died May 6, 1861, aged 75y 11m 25d	Old Section
Buchanan	Austin E.	born Oct 6, 1861, died Sep 16, 1921	Sect B

Calvary Cemetery Old and New Sections

Surname	Given Name	Description	Section
Buchanan	Edgar G.	1860-1939	Sect B
Buchanan	Eleanor Jane	wife of James Buchanan, born Apr 8, 1821, died Dec 25, 1903	Sect B
Buchanan	Ellen Elizabeth Clark	born Dec 21, 1832, died May 21, 1897	Sect B
Buchanan	Elmira	1829-1885	Sect B
Buchanan	Emma A.	dau of James and Jane Buchanan, died Sep 7, 1861, aged 8m 11d	Old Section
Buchanan	Harriet E.	dau of S.R. and N.Buchanan, died Oct 10, 1869, aged 20y 4d	Old Section
Buchanan	Hattie E. Gates	wife of FA Buchanan, Aug 18, 1865 - Jul 6, 1892	Sect B
Buchanan	James	born Feb 4, 1815, died Jan 7, 1886	Sect B
Buchanan	James F.	son of James and E J. Buchanan, died Dec 23, 1852, aged 10 months (Stone broke)	Old Section
Buchanan	James M.	died May 28, 1874 - 58y 8m 5d	Old Section
Buchanan	Jennie J.	born Oct 26, 1872, died Aug 7, 1962	Sect B
Buchanan	John	born Jan 23, 1783, died Mar 24, 1865	Old Section
Buchanan	John Clark	born Aug 11, 1859, died Nov 8, 1912	Sect B
Buchanan	John F.	son of John and Margaret Buchanan, died Mar 28, 1844, aged 19y 9m 28d	Old Section
Buchanan	John R.	died Jul 1, 1844, aged 1m 4d son of WD & LE Buchanan	Old Section
Buchanan	Julius	son of WD and LE Buchanan, died Nov 28, 1864, aged 7m 25d	Old Section
Buchanan	Katie M. Mears	wife of Edgar G. Buchanan, 1867-1901	Sect B
Buchanan	Keziah	1813-1888	Sect B
Buchanan	L. W.	died Jul 5, 1865, aged 25y 2m 5d	Old Section
Buchanan	Louisa E.	born Sep 9, 1819, died May 18, 1909	Old Section
Buchanan	Margaret	wife of John Buchanan, died Oct 14, 1852, aged 63y 10m 4d	Old Section
Buchanan	Margaret A.	1822-1887	Sect B
Buchanan	Margaret Fee	born Sep 25, 1868, died Nov 6, 1903	Sect B
Buchanan	MB	died 1813 wife of A. Buchanan (2 stones)	Old Section
Buchanan	Nancy Simmons	wife of S. Buchanan, died Sep 4, 1816, died Apr 30, 1894	Old Section
Buchanan	Nellie Clark	born Aug 4, 1866, died Mar 10, 1901	Sect B
Buchanan	Robert	born Jan 19, 1814, died Aug 30, 1891	Sect B
Buchanan	Samuel	son of Samuel and Nancy Buchanan, died Jul 2, 1853, aged 1y 5m 20d	Old Section
Buchanan	Samuel	born Nov 15, 1803, died May 3, 1886	Old Section
Buchanan	Sarah J. Ireton	wife of George M. Buchanan, 1842-1893	Old Section
Buchanan	Thomas H.	died Mar 25, 1849, son of WD & LE Buchanan, aged 7 days	Old Section
Buchanan	Tillie	born May 28, 1872, died Dec 27, 1966	Sect B
Buchanan	W. D.	died Oct 3, 1869 in 54th year of age	Old Section
Buchanan	William	died Feb 15, 1850, aged 52y 19d	Old Section
Buchannan	Margaret	wife of Andrew Buchannan, died Aug 29, 1867, aged 82y 10m 19d	Old Section
Buchannan	Samuel M.	son of WD and LE Buchannan, died Jun 23, 1860, aged 6y 3m	Old Section
Buchannon	Alexander	died May 8, 1837 in 31st year	Old Section

Calvary Cemetery Old and New Sections

Surname	Given Name	Details	Section
Buchannon	Mary	consort of Robert Buchannon died Feb 9, 1821, 40th year of age	Old Section
Buchannon	Robert	died Feb 21, 1825 - 48th year	Old Section
Buchannon	Samuel	son of Robert & Mary Buchannon, died Sep 11, 1833 in 25th year of age	Old Section
Buchanon	P	1816 handwritten	Old Section
Buchanon	unknown	Aug 17, 1806 handwritten	Old Section
Bullock	Robert L.	1913-2005	Sect A
Bullock	Rosa B.	1902-1981	Sect A
Bulow	Anna	born Oct 5, 1835, died Mar 13, 1915	Old Section
Bulow	Elizabeth	wife of Joseph Bulow, 1840-1918	Sect B
Bulow	Henrica	techter of John and Anna Bulow, born Jan 21, 1867, died Jan 16, 1879	Old Section
Bulow	John	born Apr 20, 1840, died Mar 16, 1895	Old Section
Bulow	Joseph	1842-1915	Sect B
Buntin	Peter	born Oct 17, 1805, died May 24, 1886, aged 80y 7m 7ds	Sect C
Buntin	Rebecca J.	born Nov 6, 1807, died Mar 28, 1858, aged 50y 4m 22ds	Sect C
Bureau	Carrie	wife of F. B. Bureau, Mar 21, 1871 - Oct 15, 1908	Sect A
Bureau	F. B.	Jan 25, 1865 - Apr 2, 1941	Sect A
Burns	Arthur	1884-1955	Sect A
Byrn	Elizabeth	consort of George S. Byrn, died Apr 28, 1831 - 25y	Old Section
Byrn	Emma	died Oct 27, 1840, 10 months	Old Section
Byrn	Virginia	died Aug 15, 1839 - 1y 5m	Old Section
Calvert	Lena	Aug 27, 1919 - June 25, 1999	Sect C
Calvert	Lori Marie	Sep 26, 1967 - Jul 10, 1981, dau of John and Barbara Calvert	Sect C
Camerer	Margaret	wife of Peter Camerer, dau of John and Elizabeth Powell, born Feb 15, 1828, died Mar 15, 1896	Old Section
Camerer	Peter	born Apr 23, 1821, died May 23, 1912	Old Section
Camerrer	A. M.	1849 (STONE MISSING)	Old Section
Camerrer	Elizabeth	wife of.J. Camerrer, died Jul 18, 1845 in 77th year	Old Section
Camerrer	John	died Jul 18, 1848 in 82nd year	Old Section
Camerrer	Nancy	dau of J & E Camerrer, died Sep 1, 1848 in 40th year	Old Section
Camery	Ann M.	dau of L & M Camery, died Oct 20, 1848, aged 3 years	Old Section
Camery	Clayton	son of L & M Camery, died Jan 18, 1848, aged 1y 5m 22d (STONE MISSING)	Old Section
Camery	Mary R.	dau of L & M Camery, died Aug 30, 1842, aged 8m 27d	Old Section
Camery	P.H.I.	Sep 19, 1837 (STONE MISSING)	Old Section
Camery	Poly	died Oct 26, 1821, aged 24years	Old Section
Camry	illegible		Old Section
Cann	Jessie Salt	1882-1952	Sect B
Carley	James Warren	son of Elijah and Margaret Carley, born Mar 8, 1849, died Jun 2, 1875	Old Section
Carnahan	Franklin D., Sr.	Aug 29, 1936 - Blank, wed 53 years to Katherine P.	Sect A
Carnahan	Katherine P.	Sep 24, 1936 - Jul 5, 2006	Sect A

7

Calvary Cemetery Old and New Sections

Surname	First Name	Details	Section
Carpenter	Martha J.	same as Martha J. Darling 1936-2003	Sect C
Carr	Charles M.	1857-1933	Sect D
Carr	Dan	with Guy Carr stone maybe Cox or Crane or Daniel Smith- Dora Carr's Brother Inlaw	Sect D
Carr	Dorathy	1898-1983	Sect D
Carr	Emma	wife of Charles M. Carr, 1863-1910	Sect D
Carr	W. Guy	1885-1965	Sect D
Carson	Deborah V.	Apr 26, 1961 - Jul 9, 2009, wed Mar 25, 1994 to Gary M. Carson	Sect C
Carson	Gary M.	Feb 15, 1956 - Blank, wed Mar 25, 1994 to Deborah V.	Sect C
Carson	Lee O. Kelch	Sep 30, 1927 - Sep 6, 1995, wed Apr 26, 1947 to Raymond N. Carson	Sect C
Carson	Leeola M.	Sep 30, 1927 - Sep 6, 1995, wed Apr 26, 1947	Sect C
Carson	Raymond N.	Sep 28, 1919 - Apr 20, 2008. wed Apr 26, 1947 to Lee O. Kelch	Sect C
Carson	Raymond Norman	SGT US Army WWII, Sep 28, 1919 - Apr 20, 2008, Bronze Star Medal- Combat Infantry Badge	Sect C
Cassat	Nackey Elenor	dau of Peter P & Eliza O. Cassat, died Nov 18, 1837, aged 1y 9m 21d	Old Section
Cassat	Rebecca Elizabeth	dau of Peter & Eliza Cassat, died Apr 13, 1833, aged 2y 5m 12d	Old Section
Catlett	E. Earl	1899-1965	Sect D
Catlett	Stella	1899-1965	Sect B
Caudill	Carson	Nov 29, 1935 - Blank, wed Feb 7, 1953 to Joyce	Sect C
Caudill	Charene B.	Apr 2, 1927 - Blank	Sect C
Caudill	Dellis Grant	Mar 7, 1928 - Nov 7, 1997, wed Nov 7, 1945 to Ella Grey	Sect C
Caudill	Dellis Grant	WWII, PO1 US Navy, Mar 7, 1928 - Nov 7, 1997	Sect C
Caudill	Ella Grey	Jun 28, 1929 - Sep 6, 1991, wed Nov 7, 1945 to Dellis Grant Caudill	Sect C
Caudill	Gaynell Marie Risner	Dec 26, 1922 - Mar 14, 1996, wed Nov 30, 1945 to Ishmael Caudill	Sect C
Caudill	Ishmael	Dec 12, 1921 - Nov 24, 1996, wed Nov 30, 1945 to Gaynell Marie Risner	Sect C
Caudill	James M.	Mar 7, 1926 - Mar 19, 1991	Sect C
Caudill	Joyce	Aug 10, 1932 - Jan 14, 1995, wed Feb 7, 1953 to Carson Caudill	Sect B
Caudill	Wayne	Dec 14, 1954 - Jun 24, 1955	Sect D
Caylor	Anna Parker	1854-1923	Sect D
Caylor	Caroline	1858-1949	Sect D
Caylor	George W.	1857-1950	Sect D
Caylor	Hamer	1860-1932	Sect D
Clark	Emily J.	wife of JK Clark, died Oct 24, 1888, aged 59y 7m 25d	Old Section
Clark	Larry W.	Sep 25, 1938 - Jun 25, 2010 PVT US Army	Sect C
Clark	Larry W ., Sr.	Sep 25, 1938 - Jun 25, 2010	Sect C
Clark	Lewis R.	son of JK & E.J. Clark, died Jan 15, 1861, aged 3m23d	Old Section
Clark	Nora E. Linn	Dec 28, 1920 - Blank, wed Feb 5, 1938 to Thomas S.	Sect C
Clark	Thomas S.	Jun 24, 1920 - Apr 27, 2008, wed Feb 5, 1938 to Nora E. Linn	Sect C

Calvary Cemetery Old and New Sections

Surname	Name	Details	Section
Clark	Thomas Suter	S1US Navy WWII, Jun 24, 1920 - Apr 27, 2008	Sect C
Clemons	Robert L.	Mar 2, 1957 - Apr 19, 2010	Sect B
Cochran	Casey M.	1999-1999	Sect D
Coffman	Mary	1825-1901, who lived in the family of David Moreton, Sr. for more than 50 years.	Old Section
Collins	Henry P.	son of EA and NA Collins, born Nov 22, 1835, died Sep 19, 1837	Old Section
Cooper	Augusta	wife of SH Cooper, born Jan 23, 1854, died Aug 5, 1876	Old Section
Copenhaver	Grace L.	Apr 25, 1905 - Feb 22, 1974	Sect B
Corbin	Jean Phillips	Dec 7, 1920 - Apr 7, 2007	Sect D
Cox	Berlin	Feb 28, 1910 - Jun 11, 1988	Sect D
Cox	David	Jan 15, 1944 - Sep 1, 1945, child of Berlin and Inez Cox	Sect D
Cox	Inez Carr	Oct 30, 1922 - Mar 21, 2008	Sect D
Cox	Marshall W.	1858-1919	Sect B
Cox	Phyllis	Oct 29, 1954 - Oct 31, 1954, child of Berlin and Inez Cox	Sect D
Cox	Sallie M. McMath	wife of M. W. Cox, 1867 - 19XX	Sect B
Crane	Harriet S.	1881-1962	Sect D
Crane	Margaret	1906-1984	Sect D
Crane	Walter T.	1904-1975	Sect D
Crawford	Ruth M.	1912-1948	Sect D
Crawford	Sadie Marie	Nov 22, 1913 - Sep 13, 1975	Sect A
Crawford	Sierra Mattingly	May 3, 2000.	Sect D
Crider	Kathleen	Jun 4, 1946 - Dec 16, 1997	Sect D
Croswell	Garnet L. Fancher	Sep 16, 1915 - Nov 24, 1995	Sect D
Cushard	Ada J.	1868-1951	Old Section
Cushard	Alonzo	1844-1911	Old Section
Cushard	Arbella	1847-1930	Old Section
Cushard	Benjamin F.	1867-1950	Old Section
Cushard	C. Howard	son of Ada and Benj Cushard, 1892-1974	Old Section
Cushard	Charles E.	1840-1923	Old Section
Cushard	Electra	March 11, 1956	Old Section
Cushard	Mary Staley	wife of Alonzo Cushard, 1851-1923	Old Section
Cushard	Robert	September 26, 1950	Old Section
Cushard	Sadie Sophronia	1873-1882 daughter of Alonzo and Mary Cushard	Old Section
Darling	Martha Jane	Dec 9, 1936 - Mar 15, 2003, same as Martha J. Carpenter	Sect C
Darling	Mary E.	May 14, 1937 - Blank, wed Aug 12, 1956 to William H. Darling	Sect B
Darling	Mary J.	May 20, 1910 - Feb 28, 2000, wed Dec 12, 1931 to William H. Darling	Sect B
Darling	William H.	Dec 19, 1905 - Aug 28, 1972, wed Dec 12, 1931 to Mary J.	Sect B
Darling	William H.	Jan 8, 1933 - Jul 17, 1966, wed Mary E. Aug 12, 1956	Sect B
Darling	William H. Sr.	Ohio PVT US Army, Dec 19, 1905 - Aug 27, 1972	Sect B

Calvary Cemetery Old and New Sections

Surname	Given	Details	Section
Darling	William H., Jr.	Kentucky, SFC HQ Btry 69 Fld Arty Bn, Korea, Jan 8, 1933 - Jul 16, 1966	Sect B
Daughters		died Jan 12, 1878, aged 31y 11m 16d	Old Section
Davidson	Cora H.	Feb 5, 1911 - May 4, 2005, wed Apr 24, 1928 to Roy Davidson	Sect C
Davidson	Edna	Nov 26, 1949 - Feb 18, 2008, wed Apr 17, 1965 to Tony Davidson	Sect C
Davidson	Roy	Jan 1, 1908 - Jan 13, 1994, wed Apr 24, 1928 to Cora H.	Sect C
Davidson	Tony	May 30, 1938 - Blank, wed Apr 17, 1965 to Edna	Sect C
Davis	Elsie	1881-1918	Old Section
Davis	Haydee Marie	Apr 27, 1957 - Aug 5, 1958	Sect D
Davis	Ruth Moreton	1880-1971	Sect B
Davis	Sarah R.	dau of Daniel F & Martha Davis, died Nov 3, 1838, aged 11m 25d	Old Section
Dawson	Mary O.	Aug 8, 1925 - Dec 13, 2005	Sect D
Day	I. H., MD	died 1892, aged 58years	Old Section
Day	Mary J.	wife of Dr. IH Day, born Jun 30, 1836, died May 21, 1921	Old Section
Day	Milton	son of Matthew and Mary Day, died Sep 29, 1849, aged 26y 10m 23d	Old Section
Day	Nancy E.	died 1865, aged 28 years	Sect D
Day	Nancy Lee Snider	Aug 11, 1941 - Apr 29, 2010	Sect D
Day	Roy Richard	SP4 US Army, Apr 13, 1938 - Jun 17, 2009	Old Section
Day	Samuel C.	died 1865, aged 1 year on Dr. IH Day monument	Old Section
Day	Sarah Jane Buntin Abraham	wife of Jesse W. Day, born Aug 26, 1833, died Jul 29, 1899	
Dean	Donald E.	1925-1944	Sect A
Debruler	Caroline Selby	1829-1909	Old Section
Debruler	Carrie	1869-1927	Sect D
Debruler	Cora	1880-1931	Old Section
Debruler	Elpinus Christie	1838-1921	Old Section
Debruler	R. Pearl	1879-1935	Old Section
DeLotell	Maud E.	wife of HF DeLottell, 1859-1905	Sect D
Dick	Allen G.	Jul 31, 1889 - Nov 10, 1976	Sect D
Dick	Edith L.	1888-1973	Sect D
Dick	Iva E.	Oct 9, 1893 - Oct 12, 1957	Sect D
Dick	Nettie J.	wife of William F. Dick, 1854-1908	Sect D
Dick	Walter J.	1883-1949	Sect D
Dick	William F.	1856-1929	Sect D
Dickson	Sharon	Jun 2, 1960 - Oct 10, 1979	Sect A
Dimmitt	Louisa A.	wife of M.S. Dimmitt, born 1820, died 1893	Old Section
Dimmitt	Moses S.	died May 5, 1882, aged 66y 1m 3days	Old Section
Donley	Bertha I.	dau of W. and E. Donley, born Nov 30, 1862, died Nov 3, 1865, aged 2y 11ms	Old Section
Donley	James Harry	son of William and A. Donley, born Sep 2, 1866, died Jul 21, 1890	Old Section
Downs	Alice	dau of JR and Florella Downs, died Nov 2, 1849, aged 1y 18d	Old Section

Calvary Cemetery Old and New Sections

Surname	Given Name	Details	Section
Downs	Dosier N.	1894-19XX	Sect B
Downs	Florella	wife of JR Downs and dau of John and Ann Eskham, died Oct 7, 1860, aged 29y 1m 11d	Old Section
Downs	Joseph William	no dates	Sect B
Downs	Lula M.	1891-1965	Sect B
Dufau	Brenda K. Farley	Nov 21, 1940 - Blank, wed Aug 22, 1959 to G. Glenn Dufau	Sect C
Dufau	G. Glenn	May 10, 1932 - Jun 18, 2008, wed Aug 22, 1959 to Brenda K. Farley	Sect C
Dufau	Gilbert Glenn	SGT US Marine Corp, Korea, May 10, 1932 - Jun 18, 2008	Sect C
Dunaway	Beatrice Marie	Aug 3, 1928 - Dec 5, 2009	Sect B
Dunaway	Kenneth	SN US Navy Korea, May 28, 1934 - Jun 11, 2000	Sect B
Dunaway	Larry Scott	Feb 25, 1974 - Oct 6, 2004	Sect B
Dunaway	Robert	Sp4 US Army Vietnam, Jul 14, 1947 - May 25, 1990	Sect B
Dunaway	Robert	Jul 14, 1947 - May 25, 1990	Sect B
Dunaway	Tracy B.	Mar 4, 1928 - Aug 5, 1989	Sect B
Dunaway	Vernon Scott	CM3 US Navy WWII, Nov 7, 1925 - Jun 14, 2006	Sect B
Dunaway	Vernon Scott	Nov 7, 1925 - Jun 14, 2006	Sect B
Dunbar	Angeline	wife of Robert C. Dunbar, 1827-1915	Sect A
Dunbar	Angeline	1878-1925	Sect A
Dunbar	Jimmie	son of Virginia and Ralph, Nov 14, 1940 - Mar 4, 1949	Sect A
Dunbar	Lillie	1912-1950	Sect A
Dunbar	Olga	1909-1930	Sect A
Dunbar	Ralph E.	Jul 19, 1919 - Apr 7, 1984	Sect A
Dunbar	Ralph Evans	WT3 US Navy WWII, Jul 19, 1919 - Apr 7, 1984	Sect A
Dunbar	Robert C.	1824-1903	Sect A
Dunbar	Robert C.	1865-1941	Sect A
Dunbar	Virginia	Jun 17, 1923 - Nov 4, 1968	Sect A
Dwelly	Arlene	1919-1984	Sect D
Dwelly	James Roger	PSG US Army Vietnam, Jul 14, 1935 - Jul 15, 1999	Sect C
Dwelly	Jimmy	Jul 14, 1935 - Jul 15, 1999	Sect C
Dwelly	Leroy J.	1913-1984	Sect D
Dwelly	Margaret Alline East	Aug 10, 1938 - Blank, wed Feb 25, 1956 to James R. Dwelly	Sect C
East	Nancy M.	Feb 20, 1955 - Jun 3, 1995	Sect B
Eckart	Eugene	1918-1974	Sect D
Eckart	Kathryn	1914-1996	Sect D
Eckart	Keith	Jun 28 1931 - Dec 31, 1993, wed Mar 9, 1956 to Rita	Sect D
Eckart	Rita	Jul 31, 1936 - Blank, wed Mar 9, 1956 to Keith Eckart	Sect D
Edmondson	Leisa Ann	Mar 5, 1958 - Jul 17, 2003	Sect C
Edwards	Irene	1908-1996	Sect A
Edwards	William Helbert	1900-1971	Sect A

Calvary Cemetery Old and New Sections

Surname	Given Name	Dates / Information	Section
Ellis	Alta	1896-1996	Sect D
Ellis	Floyd	1890-1977	Sect D
Erdman	Janet L.	1935-1966	Sect D
Erdman	Reichert B.	1936-Blank	Sect D
Eskam	John	a native of England, died Oct 22, 1847 in 69th year of his age (STONE MISSING)	Old Section
Estep	Douglas A.	Feb 13, 1960 - Jun 5, 1980	Sect D
Estep	Infant	February 25, 1959	Sect D
Estep	Leo J.	May 3, 1937 - Blank, wed Jun 2, 1956 to Ona Lee	Sect D
Estep	Ona Lee	Oct 14, 1938 - Blank, wed Jun 2, 1956 to Leo J. Estep	Sect D
Fancher	A. Eliza	1863-1940	Sect D
Fancher	Arthur	1886-1970	Sect D
Fancher	B. F.	1884-1910	Sect D
Fancher	Edward C.	1880-1932	Sect D
Fancher	Elsie	wife of Libeus Fancher, 1815-1879	Old Section
Fancher	Enos	1863-1895, 32 years	Sect A
Fancher	John	1835-1905	Old Section
Fancher	Maria	wife of John Fancher, 1832-1889	Old Section
Fancher	Nora E.	1888-1970	Sect D
Fancher	Pearl B.	1876-1971	Sect D
Fancher	Thomas C.	1857-1942	Sect D
Faubion	Alberta M.	Sep 27, 1905 - Jan 31, 1987	Sect C
Faubion	Edgar M.	Mar 22, 1908 - Apr 27, 1970	Sect C
Faubion	Edgar M.	OH PVT Infantry WWII, Mar 22, 1908 - Apr 27, 1970	Sect C
Faulkner	James Allen	1998-1998	Sect B
Fee	A. C.	Monument	Sect B
Fee	Alonzo C.	1850-1921	Sect B
Fee	Anna B.	1851-1934	Sect B
Fee	Anna Louise	dau of JM & SM Fee, died Aug 6, 1888, aged 4m 8ds	Sect B
Fee	Augustus	son of Thomas and Helen Fee, died Feb 24, 1834 - 11months	Old Section
Fee	Augustus E.	son of Thomas and Helen Fee, died Jul 28, 1830, aged 2y 9m 22d	Old Section
Fee	Ethel Estella	dau of DW & Lizzie Fee, born Aug 12, 1883, died Nov 3, 1884	Sect D
Fee	G.E.N.	Feb 1836. (STONE MISSING)	Old Section
Fee	Jessie	1873-1914	Sect B
Fee	Kathleen E. Hiles	Jun 8, 1948 - Oct 21, 2009	Sect C
Feldkamp	Richard L., Sr.	Oct 16, 1946 - Blank	Sect C
Fenton	Ann Eliza	wife of William E. Fenton, died Aug 3, 1871, aged 26y 3m 15d	Old Section
Fisher	Alice E.	dau of WE and Etna Fisher, born Oct 6, 1880, died Sep 19, 1882, 1 year 11 months	Old Section

Calvary Cemetery Old and New Sections

Surname	Given Name	Details	Section
Fisher	Benjamin	1861-1920	Sect D
Fisher	Benjamin F.	born Dec 19, 1827, died Sep 21, 1900	Old Section
Fisher	Delilah	born Oct 7, 1820, died Aug 16, 1875	Old Section
Fisher	Ediczene Selby	wife of BF Fisher, died Nov 23, 1876, aged 54y 11m 28d	Old Section
Fisher	Elizabeth	wife of Peter Fisher, died Jan 31, 1843, 48 years	Old Section
Fisher	George E.	1889-1938	Sect D
Fisher	Helen	born Jul 19, 1887, died May 26, 1889, dau of WE & E Fisher	Old Section
Fisher	James M.	son of BF & EZ Fisher, died Feb 27, 1852, aged 5mo. 2ds	Old Section
Fisher	Jessie I.	1890-1972	Sect D
Fisher	Lou E.	born Mar 20, 1883, died May 1, 1889, child of WE & E Fisher	Old Section
Fisher	Lucille S. Shields	Dec 21, 1951-Blank, wed Sep 22, 1972 to Paul Michael Fisher	Sect D
Fisher	Maria	born Aug 19, 1856, died Sep 8, 1875	Old Section
Fisher	Paul Michael	US Marine Corps Vietnam, Jul 21, 1949 - May 10, 2001	Sect D
Fisher	Paul Michael	Jul 21, 1949 - May 10, 2001, wed Sep 22, 1972 to Lucille S. Fisher	Sect D
Fisher	Peter	died Aug 18, 1869, agee 84 years	Old Section
Fisher	Sarah C.	wife of Benjamin Fisher, 1862-1937	Sect D
Fisher	Truman	son of DY & D Fisher, died Sep 29, 1879, aged 18y 2m 12d	Old Section
Fletcher	Charles	1883-1964	Sect D
Fletcher	George L.	1861-1938	Sect B
Fletcher	Howard F.	1897-1904	Sect B
Fletcher	Jane	wife of Thomas Fletcher, born May 6, 1823, died Nov 15, 1911	Sect B
Fletcher	Jennie	wife of W. R. Fletcher, 1853-1938	Sect D
Fletcher	John H.	son of WR & Jennie Fletcher, 1890-1908	Sect D
Fletcher	Mary	1889-1971	Sect B
Fletcher	Mary V.	1900-1903	Sect B
Fletcher	May C.	1862-1924	Sect B
Fletcher	Stanley L.	1893-1970	Sect D
Fletcher	Stanley L.	OH CPL Co. E. 146 Inf. WWI, Aug 11, 1893 - Nov 10, 1970	Sect B
Fletcher	Thomas	born Aug 17, 1817, died May 12, 1896	Sect B
Fletcher	W. R.	1852-1944	Sect D
Fletcher	William	son of John and Eliza Fletcher, died Jul 1, 1848, aged 3m 17d	Old Section
Flik	blank	1816 (handwritten)	Old Section
Foley	Cranston	1954-2009	Sect B
Foley	Irvin W.	Oct 8, 1968 - Sep 27, 2009, wod cross and separate stone	Sect B
Ford	Elizabeth	wife of Abram Ford, died Aug 13, 1859, aged 41y 3m 28d	Old Section
Forste	Carolyn S.	1948-2012	Sect C
Forste	Joseph T.	1990-2011, wood cross and funeral home marker	Sect C
Forsythe	Sophronia A. Staley	1832-1908	Old Section

13

Calvary Cemetery Old and New Sections

Surname	Given	Info	Section
Frank	Consuelo	1907-1907	Sect B
Frank	Josephine D.	1873-19XX	Sect B
Frank	Mable	1893-1895	Sect B
Frank	Mary E.	1857-1903	Sect B
Frank	William L.	1859-1934	Sect B
Frazier	Flavious J.	died Jun 23, 1850, aged 33y 4m 2d	Old Section
Friend	Robert B.	1899-1955	Sect D
Friend	S. K.	born Jul 15, 1871, died Jan 5, 1928, aged 56y 5m 21ds	Sect D
Friend	Sallie	1907-1934	Sect D
Fulton	C. Douglas	Jan 23, 1967 - Nov 16, 2009	Sect D
Gates	Anna (maybe)	1907-1908 - 2 months	Sect A
Gates	Homer	born Mar 18, 1883, died Mar 19, 1883, son of JH & JF Gates	Sect A
Gates	Jimmy	no dates	Sect A
Gates	John	born Jan 4, 1884 - Jan 5, 1884, son of JH & JF Gates	Sect A
Gaylor	John O.	son of George & Martha Gaylor, born Jan 8, 1868, died Dec 12, 1874 (illegible)	Old Section
Gaylor	Thomas P.	son of George and Martha Gaylor, died Feb 16, 1857 - 3 months (illegible)	Old Section
Gilbert	Ann	consort of Rev. Micah Gilbert, died Sep 10, 1831 in 66th year	Old Section
Gilbert	Micah, Rev.	died Jul 1, 1833 in 78th year	Old Section
Gilfillen	George A.	son of JG & SG Gilfillen, died Sep 17, 1852, aged 12y 4m 13d	Old Section
Gilfillen	John G.	died Oct 5, 1875, aged 70y 11m 21d	Old Section
Gilfillen	monument	monument	Sect D
Gilfillen	Samuel	child of JG & S Gilfillen, died Jun 11, 1852	Old Section
Gilfillen	Sarah B.	died Jan 30, 1888, aged 76	Old Section
Gilfillen	Sarah G,	child of JG & S Gilfillen, died Jun 27, 1863, aged 12y 2m 2d	Old Section
Gilfillen	W. L.	child of JG & S Gilfillen died Feb 15, 1847, aged 1y 1m 1d	Old Section
Gilfillen	William T.	son of JG & S Gilfillen, died Dec 17, 1880, aged 42y 11m 20d	Old Section
Glaser	Catherine	1860-1936	Sect B
Glaser	Howard	1889-1960	Sect B
Gorth	Bertha V.	1894-1950	Sect D
Gorth	Hazel Kocher	Dec 26, 1932 - Jun 17, 2004	Sect D
Gorth	Henry J.	1893-1966	Sect D
Gorth	Infant	no dates	Sect D
Gorth	Jean M.	1934-2000	Sect C
Gorth	Joe L.	1941 - Blank	Sect C
Gorth	Joseph I.	Oct 5, 1921 - Jun 6, 1998	Sect D
Gorth	Joseph I.	PVT US Army WWII, Oct 5, 1921 - Jun 6, 1998	Sect D
Gorth	Lena Sparks	Aug 28, 1889 - Jun 3, 1967	Sect D
Gorth	Linda S.	1948 - Blank, wed Feb 8, 1967 to Russell A. Gorth	Sect D

Calvary Cemetery Old and New Sections

Surname	Given Name	Details	Section
Gorth	Russell A.	OH Sgt US Army Vietnam, Jan 30, 1945 - Apr 6, 1974	Sect D
Gorth	Russell A.	1945-1974, wed Feb 8, 1967 to Linda S.	Sect D
Gorth	Teresa J.	Jan 20, 1953 - Nov 19, 1996	Sect D
Gorth	Thelma L.	Mar 19, 1921 - Apr 2, 1996	Sect D
Gorth	Virginia R.	1923-1989	Sect D
Gorth	William L.	1930 - Blank	Sect D
Green	Andrew B.	son of Henry and Carolina Green, born Oct 8, 1860, died Mar 23, 1862	Old Section
Green	Ashley M.	Mar 2, 1989 - Apr 22, 1989	Sect B
Gregg	Caroline N.	dau of George and Sarah Gregg, born Dec 9, 1820, died Apr 15, 1840, aged 19y 4m 6days	Old Section
Gregg	Elizabeth	wife of Hiran D. Gregg, born Dec 11, 1807, died Dec 4, 1887	Old Section
Gregg	George	born Mar 25, 1790, died Jan 12, 1862	Old Section
Gregg	Hiram D.	born Sep 16, 1805, died Feb 17, 1890	Old Section
Gregg	Hiram F.	1849-1923	Sect D
Gregg	Infant	Daughter of Hiram and Elizabeth, born Jan 29, 1841, died Jul 29, 1841	Old Section
Gregg	Infant	Sons of Hiram and Elizabeth Gregg, born Jan 21, 1840, died Jan 22 and 23, 1840	Old Section
Gregg	John	infant son of George and Sarah Gregg, died Jul 23, 1826	Old Section
Gregg	Nellie A.	1874-19XX	Sect D
Gregg	S. Frances	1851-1907	Sect D
Gregg	Sarah Ann	dau of George and Sarah Gregg, born Jan 15, 1819, died Mar 25, 1828, aged 9y 2m 11ds	Old Section
Gregg	Stanley	1874-1901	Sect D
Grey	Alice Abrams	1869-1961	Sect D
Groppenbacher	Elizabeth	wife of Henry Groppenbacher, Jun 15, 1854 - Aug 2, 1918	Sect D
Groppenbacher	Henry	Jul 2, 1847 - Jan 4, 1923	Sect D
Groppenbacher	Henry	1877-1948	Sect D
Groppenbacher	Jacob	1881-1959	Sect D
Groppenbacher	Katie	1883-1970	Sect D
Groves	Georgana	1881-1971	Sect A
Gwynn	Julia Ann	dau of J & H Gwynn, died Sep 30, 1843, aged 8y 7m 22d	Old Section
Haas	Bennie R.	1913 - 1956	Sect D
Haas	N. Marie O'Neal Gorth	Jun 30, 1919 - Sep 18, 2001	Sect D
Hackney	Jeffery L.	1979-2005	Sect D
Hall	Arthur	Ohio CPL Co. G. 146 Infantry, WWI, Apr 1, 1888 - Feb 1, 1968	Old Section
Hall	B. M.	1841-1912	Sect B
Hall	Elmer	son of JT and Henrietta Hall, born Jan 26, 1877, died Sep 11, 1887	Old Section
Hall	F. C.	1843-1911	Sect B
Hall	Henrietta	wife of JT Hall, born Dec 18, 1857, died Dec 2, 1899	Old Section

15

Calvary Cemetery Old and New Sections

Surname	Given		Old Section
Hall	John Thomas	May 25, 1854 - Feb 16, 1920	Sect C
Hamilton	Logan Curtis	Sep 25, 2007, son of Steven and Julianne	Sect D
Hampton	Michael A.	Feb 3, 1986 - Oct 22, 2004	Sect D
Hampton	Richard C.	Jul 10, 1943 - Blank	Sect B
Haney	Bessie	Apr 17, 1918 - May 21, 2011, wed Oct 21, 1943 to Iron Haney	Sect B
Haney	Clifford D.	1922-1987	Sect B
Haney	Etta M.	1916-2008	Sect B
Haney	Iron	Dec 2, 1923 - Jun 15, 1995, wed Oct 21, 1943 to Bessie	Sect A
Hannah	Eulah M.	1904-1980	Sect D
Hannah	Georgia H.	1866-1951	Sect A
Hannah	Harry L.	1904-1976	Sect D
Hannah	Harvie	1827-1906	Sect C
Hannah	Hattie	1895-1981	Sect C
Hannah	John William	US Navy, May 4, 1934 - Feb 21, 1987	Sect C
Hannah	John William	May 4, 1934 - Feb 21, 1987	Old Section
Hannah	Louie C.	dau of AH & MJ Hannah, born Nov 16, 1864, died Jan 6, 1881, aged 18y 1m 21d	Sect D
Hannah	Mary J.	1834-1915	Sect C
Hannah	Samuel J.	1899-1969	Sect A
Harover	June	May 3, 1942 - Blank, wed Dec 6, 1962 to Virgil E. Harover	Sect A
Harover	Virgil Edwin	SP4 US Army, Korea, Sep 14, 1937 - Sep 23, 2006	Sect A
Harover	Virgil Edwin	Sep 14, 1937 - Sep 23, 2006, wed Dec 6, 1962 to June	Sect D
Harris	Mary K.	Nov 27, 1941 - Dec 16, 2001, wed Jun 30, 1971 to William R.	Sect D
Harris	William R.	PFC US Army WWII, Nov 27, 1923 - Jun 14, 1999	Sect D
Harris	William R.	Nov 27, 1923 - Jun 14, 1999, wed Jun 30, 1971 to Mary K.	Sect A
Hawk	Anderson I.	1848-1896	Sect A
Hawk	John	1870 - 1940 (born May 9, 1870, died Jun 27, 1940, son of A.I. and Sarah Hawk)	Sect A
Hawk	Minnie	1882-1967	Sect A
Hawk	Sarah	1849-1944	Sect A
Hawkins	Roberta Lynn	1951-1986	Sect C
Hayden	Charles S.	Jan 6, 1939 - Aug 27, 2000	Sect D
Hayden	Chester	Apr 10, 1907 - Feb 6, 2004, wed May 7, 1931 to Olive M.	Sect D
Hayden	Olive M.	May 11, 1914 - Jul 24, 2005, wed May 7, 1931 to Chester Hayden	Sect D
Hazenfeld	Jeffrey Laine	Jan 24, 1955 - Jun 3, 2003	Sect C
Head	Larkin O.	1901-1987, wed Sep 21, 1925 to Lola M.	Sect B
Head	Lola M.	1901-1986, wed Sep 21, 1925 to Larkin O. Head	Sect B
Helton	Arbie C.	1912-1955	Sect D
Helton	Beecher F.	PFC US Army WWII, Nov 24, 1919 - Jul 26, 1996	Sect C
Helton	Beecher F.	Nov 24, 1919 - Jul 26, 1996	Sect C

Calvary Cemetery Old and New Sections

Surname	First Name	Details	Section
Helton	Dudley	1886-1967	Sect D
Henize	Emilie C.	Jun 16, 1936 - Jan 9, 1991	Sect A
Hensley	Alfred	PFC US Army WWII, Oct 26, 1922 - Sep 3, 1999	Sect C
Hensley	Alfred	Oct 26, 1922 - Sep 3, 1999	Sect C
Hensley	Alvin W.	Jul 3, 1951 - May 4, 2001	Sect C
Hensley	Annie	Nov 22, 1929 - Blank	Sect C
Hensley	Daisy A. Hudson	Oct 27, 1929 - Oct 15, 1991, wed Oct 5, 1946 to Earl Hensley	Sect C
Hensley	Earl	Oct 13, 1924 - May 1, 1997, wed Oct 5, 1946 to Daisy A. Hudson	Sect C
Hensley	Earl	PFC US Army Air Forces WWII, Oct 13, 1924 - May 1, 1997	Sect C
Hensley	Paul	US Army Dec 8, 1927 - Aug 26, 2007	Sect C
Hensley	Raleigh	Feb 12, 1919 - May 23, 1991	Sect C
Hensley	Raleigh	Tec 5 US Army WWII, Feb 12, 1919 - May 23, 1991	Sect C
Hensley	Sarah	Nov 5, 1925 - Aug 31, 1986	Sect C
Hetterick	Charles E.	PFC US Army WWII, PURPLE HEART, Aug 30, 1924 - May 6, 2006	Sect C
Hetterick	Charles E.	1924-2006	Sect C
Hetterick	Debra S. Tudor	May 28, 1957 - Mar 2, 1997	Sect C
Hetterick	Hannah Marie	Sep 15, 1994 - infant daughter	Sect C
Hetterick	John E.	Jun 12, 1957 - Blank	Sect C
Hetterick	Joshua	infant son of John E. and Debra S. Hetterick, Nov 6, 1978	Sect C
Hetterick	Margaret E.	1926-1970	Sect D
Hiatt	Everett E.	Mar 27, 1903 - Apr 25, 1988	Sect D
Hiatt	Margaret H. Kinnett	Oct 2, 1905 - Apr 19, 1994	Sect D
Hick	Hezakiah	died Mar 6, 1852, aged 36y 2m 9d	Old Section
Hiles	Dorothy Ann	May 10, 1939 - Blank	Sect C
Hiles	Hazel M.	Jun 22, 1922 - Mar 28, 2002	Sect C
Hiles	Herman D.	MM2 US Navy WWII, Apr 4, 1907 - Nov 20, 1998	Sect C
Hiles	Herman D.	1907-1998	Sect C
Hiles	Infant	Infant son of Herman and Nellie Mae Hiles, Feb 2, 1931	Sect D
Hiles	Keith D.	Mar 6, 1960 - Mar 3, 1988	Sect C
Hiles	Larry Gene	Oct 5, 1938 - Apr 28, 1997	Sect C
Hiles	Nellie Mae	1908-1986	Sect C
Hiles	Richard	F1 US Coast Guard, WWII, Apr 23, 1928 - Feb 21, 1985	Sect C
Hiles	Richard Daniel	Dec 17, 1952 - May 6, 1996	Sect C
Hill	Josephine C.	dau of N & M A Hill, died Nov 13, 1863, aged 14y 4m 8d	Old Section
Hill	Luella J.	wife of Thomas G. Hill, May 30, 1854 - Mar 17, 1943	Old Section
Hill	Mary A.	wife of Nicholas Hill, 1823-1908	Old Section
Hill	Nicholas	1820-1876	Old Section
Hill	Nicholas Harvey	Apr 16, 1875 - Sep 20, 1910	Old Section

Calvary Cemetery Old and New Sections

Surname	Given Name	Details	Section
Hill	Roy	son of Thomas and Luella Hill, born Jun 4, 1885, died Feb 18, 1896	Old Section
Hill	Susanna A.	dau of N & M A Hill, died Oct 6, 1864, aged 14y 7m 15d	Old Section
Hill	Thomas G.	Nov 8, 1846 - Aug 6, 1928	Old Section
Hines	Elizabeth	consort of James T. Hines, died May 19, 1848, aged 25y 5m 4d	Old Section
Hines	James T.	died Oct 28, 1848, aged 32y 11m 3d	Old Section
Hines	Nathaniel	died Dec 21, 1844, 80 yrs of age	Old Section
Hitch	Aristides	son of Nackey Elen and Thos. Hitch, died Sep 5, 1838, aged 1y 1m	Old Section
Hitch	Nackey	wife of William Hitch, died Jul 14, 1849, aged 42 years	Old Section
Hitch	Nackey Elen	wife of Thomas Hitch, died Aug 27, 1838, 23rd yr	Old Section
Hitch	William H. H. H.	son of William and Nackey Hitch, died Sep 2, 1837, 11m 25d	Old Section
Hix	Ileen T. Gorth	Sep 5, 1923 - Jun 11, 1995	Sect D
Ho******	D	Apr 5, 1818 (handwritten)	Old Section
Hobbs	Christine	1923-1938	Sect D
Hoggan	James M.	born 1815, died 1892	Old Section
Hoggan	Mary G.	born 1819, died 1899	Old Section
Hoggan	William S.	born 1855, died 1872	Old Section
Holland	Andy	1890-1908	Sect D
Holland	Clarence	1884-1962	Sect D
Holland	Clarence, Jr.	US Army WWII, Jan 4, 1924 - Jul 18, 1999	Sect D
Holland	E. Florence	1867-1942	Sect B
Holland	Elmer	son of William and Louise Holland, 1893-1894	Sect B
Holland	Eugene S.	PVT US Army, Korea, Sep 26, 1933 - Jul 18, 1996	Sect C
Holland	Eugene Stratton	Sep 26, 1933 - Jul 18, 1996, wed Jun 30, 1956 to Joann Hiles	Sect C
Holland	Gordon D.	OH S1 USNR WWII, Dec 21, 1910 - May 14, 1973	Sect A
Holland	Harriet E.	1918-1994	Sect A
Holland	Joann Hiles	May 17, 1936 - Blank, wed June 30, 1956 to Eugene Stratton Holland	Sect C
Holland	Josephine	1871-1962	Sect B
Holland	Louise	wife of William Holland, 1866-1926	Sect B
Holland	Meredith E.	1917-1977	Sect A
Holland	Ruth E.	Mar 7, 1933 - Feb 19, 1994	Sect D
Holland	Stella	wife of Clarence Holland, 1888-1962	Sect D
Holland	William	1863-1932	Sect B
Holland	Zackariah	Oct 21, 1837 - Dec 20, 1903	Sect D
Holman	David William	Jul 23, 1950 - Jun 14, 1970	Sect B
Holman	Edith M. Warden	May 5, 1928 - May 16, 2008, wed Jun 8, 1947 to Roy W. Holman	Sect A
Holman	Jeffrey Joe	Oct 25, 1953 - May 24, 1983	Sect D
Holman	Michael T.	Mar 21, 1948 - Sep 3, 2002	Sect B
Holman	Roy W.	Sep 21, 1926 - Blank, wed Jun 8, 1947 to Edith M. Warden	Sect B

Calvary Cemetery Old and New Sections

Surname	Given Name	Details	Section
Holter	Augustus	son of John D. and Anna Holter, died Sep 18, 1843, aged 2y 6d	Old Section
Holter	Augustus W.	son of LP and TH Holter, died Jul 15, 1864, aged 16y 10m 29d	Old Section
Holter	Eliza E.	dau of BF & EM Holter, died Jul 25, 1865, aged 3m 26d	Old Section
Holter	Eliza M.	wife of BF Holter, died Jun 26, 1865, aged 27y 6m 14d	Old Section
Holter	George W.	son of John and MA Holter died Jan 30, 1840, aged 22y 1m 4d	Old Section
Holter	Mary A.	wife of John D Holter, born 1782, died Dec 1866, aged 84 years, 2 stones	Old Section
Holter	Nelson L.	born Dec 2, 1808, died Feb 27, 1889	Old Section
Holter	Rhoda J.	wife of W. H. Holter, born Feb 11, 1830, died Apr 1, 1909	Old Section
Holter	Thomas F.	son of Lawson P and Thursa A. Holter, died July 2, 1860 - aged 27y 1m 4ds	Old Section
Holter	W. H.	died Dec 27, 1899, aged 84y 5m 27d	Old Section
Holter	Willie Grant	son of BF and EM Holter, died Dec 6, 1863, aged 6m 21d	Old Section
Holton	Donald John	1955-1971	Sect D
Holton	Donald W.	1928-1980	Sect D
Holton	Effie Harmon	1901-1992	Sect D
Holton	Elizabeth	1873-1958	Sect D
Holton	Jean	1927-1971	Sect D
Holton	Mary Jo	1930-1962	Sect D
Holton	Noble Steen	1902-1965	Sect D
Holton	Virginia E. White	Mar 8, 1930 - May 17, 2006	Sect D
Holton	Wayne M.	1868-1959	Sect D
Holton	Wayne T.	Nov 12, 1926 - Jun 18, 1996	Sect D
Holton	Wayne Thomas	Cox US Navy WWII, Nov 12, 1926 - Jun 18, 1996	Sect D
Hopkins	Emma Norris	wife of A. D. Hopkins, 1849-1904	Old Section
Houser	America E.	1843-1905	Sect B
Houser	Samuel M.	1835-1913	Sect B
Housh	Emmer H.	1869-1958	Sect B
Housh	Euphemia	1884-1917	Sect D
Housh	Laura B.	1871-1963	Sect B
Housh	Samuel D.	1856-1924	Sect D
Housh	Sarah E.	1839-1922	Sect D
Housh	William G.	1832-1913	Sect D
Houston	Arvena D.	wife of W. S. Houston, 1866-1923	Sect D
Houston	George	1893-1963	Sect D
Houston	Sarah Abram	1891-1925	Sect B
Houston	W. S.	1865-1933	Sect D
Howard	Abner R.	1834-1900	Sect B
Howard	James M.	1867-1937	Sect B
Howard	Mary Ann	1836-1930	Sect B

19

Calvary Cemetery Old and New Sections

Surname	First Name	Info	Section
Howard	Vintson F.	1879-1903	Sect B
Howard	Zella Gertrude	1873-1950	Sect B
Hughes	Ella	1872-1955	Sect C
Hughes	Floyd	1909-1966	Sect C
Hughes	Henry N.	Mar 3, 1873 - Aug 11, 1924	Sect C
Hughes	Margaret	1912-1982	Sect C
Hull	Betty	April 20, 1932 - Blank	Sect B
Hull	Daris Dwayne	Dec 1, 1975 - Mar 21, 2011	Sect D
Hull	Ida M.	1908-1987	Sect D
Hull	Jerry Lee	Mar 12, 1958 - Dec 7, 1989, wed Oct 5, 1982 to Rita Kay	Sect B
Hull	John W.	1898-1965	Sect D
Hull	Kenneth E.	Sep 1, 1927 - Jan 21, 1929	Sect D
Hull	Louella L.	May 27, 1942 - Mar 2, 2007, wed Feb 19, 1959 to Robert R. Hull	Sect D
Hull	Rita Kay	Nov 21, 1962 - Blank, wed Oct 5, 1982 to Jerry Lee Hull	Sect B
Hull	Robert R.	Sep 30, 1931 - Blank, wed Feb 19, 1959 to Louella L.	Sect D
Hull	Roger W.	Sep 15, 1970 - Apr 19, 2001	Sect B
Hull	Todd A.	1967-2011	Sect D
Hull	William	Jul 31, 1924 - Sep 30, 2003	Sect B
Hundley	Margaret E.	wife of William M. Hundley, Oct 27, 1867-Jun 21, 1906	Sect A
Ibendorf	Maria	born Feb 13, 1833, in Retschon, Mechlenburg, Schwerin, died Feb 10, 1889, 55y 11m 2 ds	Old Section
illegible	Frank H.	footstone in plot between Daughters and Mary Coffman or Morton Lot	Old Section
illegible	illegible	Jan 15, 185X	Old Section
Ireton	Martha E.	dau of Samuel and Nancy Ireton, died Jan 21, 1855, aged 5m 10d	Old Section
Ireton	Nancy M.	wife of Samuel Ireton, died Feb 19, 1873, aged 55y 2m 24d	Old Section
Ireton	Rolin	died Dec 23, 1847 in 71st year of his age	Old Section
Ireton	Samuel	born Oct 1, 1812, died Apr 15, 1889	Old Section
Ireton	Samuel Edey	son of Samuel and Nancy M. Ireton, died Sep 11, 1860, aged 4m 14d	Old Section
Ireton	Sarah	wife of Rolin Ireton, died Oct 15, 1854, aged 72y 2m	Old Section
J	MJ	Jy 17, 1810 handwritten	Old Section
Jefferson	Beverly S.	1947-1968	Sect D
Jefferson	Jesse J.	1902-1948	Sect D
Johnson	Charles	1886-1959	Sect A
Johnson	Charles	KY PVT US Army WW1, Oct 20, 1885 - Oct 17, 1959	Sect A
Johnson	Fred L.	OH PFC Co. E 120 Inf. Regt WWII, July 12, 1921 - Apr 22, 1971	Sect A
Johnson	Oley A.	1898-1973	Sect A
Jones	Anna S.	1887-1966	Sect D
Jones	Billie	Feb 12, 1912 - Apr 23, 2001, wed Feb 22, 1934 to Nola	Sect C
Jones	Celia A.	dau of G & E Jones, died May 20, 1870, aged 18y 4m	Old Section

Calvary Cemetery Old and New Sections

Surname	Given Name	Details	Section
Jones	Charles F.	1907-1975	Sect D
Jones	Cora B. Dick	1881-1941	Sect D
Jones	David F.	1884-1976	Sect D
Jones	Edythe O.	1908-1995	Sect D
Jones	Mary H.	wife of Thomas Jones, died Nov 18, 1899, aged 61y 4d (monument turned face down - tornado 2012)	Sect B
Jones	Mother	on Jones Lot	Sect B
Jones	Nola	Feb 16, 1918 - Blank, wed Feb 22, 1934 to Billie Jones	Sect C
Jones	R	no dates(recorded by DAR STONE MISSING)	Old Section
Jones	Thomas	died Mar 23, 1914 aged 81y 23d,(monument turned face down - tornado 2012)	Sect B
Joslen	Hannah	dau of Israel and Mary Joslin, died Aug 17, 1838, aged 2y 2m 8d	Old Section
Kaucher	Hattie M.	1891-1976	Sect B
Kaucher	Henry J.	1887-1949	Sect B
Keller	Emma	dau of Emanuel & Theakla Keller, born Apr 9, 1887, died Jul 18, 1887	Sect C
Keller	John	born 1815, died Apr 14, 1887 - 72 years	Sect C
Keller	Victoria	wife of John Keller, born Jul 9, 1825, died Dec 20, 1886, aged 61y 5m 11ds	Sect C
Kennedy	Georgia M.	born Feb 28, 1891, no death date	Old Section
Kennedy	Roy E.	born Feb 25, 1885, died Dec 24, 1941, aged 56y 9m 29ds	Old Section
Kerber	Jacob	1830-1903	Sect D
Kerber	Katharine Gammer	wife of Jacob Kerber, 1837-1919	Sect D
Kerber	Mother	next to Jacob and Katherine Kerber	Sect D
Kidd	Raymond W., Jr.	Jul 17, 1973 - Nov 7, 1988	Sect A
Kinnett	Ermina J.	dau of James and Minnie Kinnett, 1897-1918	Sect D
Kinnett	James	1857-1941	Sect D
Kinnett	Lilly	1901-1981, dau of James and Minnie Kinnett	Sect D
Kinnett	Minnie E.	wife of James Kinnett, 1869-1946	Sect D
Kinsey	Jennette	1857-1952	Sect B
Kinsey	Jesse M.	1856-1945	Sect B
Kinzer	Betty M.	1924-1992, wed Aug 2, 1941 to Charles J. Kinzer	Sect A
Kinzer	Charles J.	1920-1983, wed Aug 2, 1941 to Betty M.	Sect A
Kinzer	Charles J.	CPL US Army WWII, Mar 5, 1920 - Feb 26, 1983	Sect A
Koltebah	George F.	Sep 24, 1864 - Nov 12, 1943	Sect A
Koltebah	May E.	Oct 7, 1872 - Jun 3, 1938	Sect A
Lamb	Francile	Jul 19, 1895 - Jul 12, 1969	Sect C
Lane	Alice Edna	born Nov 24, 1867, died Feb 8, 1868	Old Section
Lane	Claude	(little Claude) son of M & C Lane, born Sep 3, 1875 (no death date)	Old Section
Lane	John F.	died Dec 14, 1882, aged 52y 11m 13d	Old Section

Calvary Cemetery Old and New Sections

Surname	Given Name	Details	Section
Lane	Mary Louisa	died Jan 19, 1906, aged 70y 3m 22d	Old Section
Larrison	Catherine	Sep 24, 1923 - Blank, wed Jul 2, 1938 to Elwood Larrison	Sect B
Larrison	Elwood	Mar 19, 1915 - May 13, 1995, wed Jul 2, 1938 to Catherine	Sect B
Lauderman	Mary E.	Jan 7, 1914 - Mar 5, 1994	Sect B
Laycock	Eugene	1892-1946	Old Section
Laycock	Mary O.	1889-1942	Old Section
Laycock	Olive C.	infant dau of E & MO Laycock, Jul 31, 1917	Old Section
Leach	Melvina	wife of S. R. Leach, 1860-1914	Sect D
Leach	Ruth E.	1896-1980	Sect D
Leach	S. R.	1859-1944	Sect D
Leach	Thurman A.	1892-1942	Sect D
Lemar	Carrie	1877-1928	Old Section
Lemar	Clara E.	1877-1935	Sect A
Lemar	Granville	son of James and Rachel G. Lemar, 1882, aged 14d	Old Section
Lemar	Herbert K.	1905-1959	Sect D
Lemar	James	1852-1917	Old Section
Lemar	Jeannette	1909-1993	Sect D
Lemar	Lewa J.	1879-1973	Sect A
Lemar	Rachel G.	wife of James, 1854-1939	Old Section
Lemar	Robert K.	US Army, Jul 22, 1934 - Sep 8, 1995	Sect D
Lemar	Robert K.	Jul 22, 1934 - Sep 8, 1995, wed Jun 2, 1956 to (blank)	Sect D
Leslie	Aydelotte	Nov 19, 1887 - Dec 10, 1963	Sect A
Leslie	Esther A.	May 17, 1889 - Mar 4, 1990	Sect A
Levi	Eliza J.	dau of Willis and Huld Levi, died May 10 1853, aged 25 days	Old Section
Liebich	C. F. (Charlie)	1864-1945	Sect B
Liebich	Elizabeth	1861-1930	Sect B
Liebich	Martin	son of Stephen and Caroline Liebich, born Mar 22, 1862, died Aug 9, 1896	Sect B
Liming	Roy Franklin	Oct 29, 1928 - Feb 21, 1997	Sect C
Littleton	Catherine	born Mar 9, 1791, died Aug 2, 1871	Old Section
Littleton	Thomas	born Mar 22, 1789, died Aug 12, 1874	Old Section
Logan	Charles R.	BOSN US Coast Guard WWII, Aug 3, 1908 - Aug 24, 1978	Sect C
Logan	Charles R.	1908-1978	Sect C
Logan	Inez M.	1918-1997	Sect C
Lough	Bart	Sep 12, 1837 (STONE MISSING)	Old Section
Lowe	Julia E.	1943-Blank	Sect B
Lowe	Palmer K.	1940-1994	Sect B
Luck	Fannie M.	1842-1913	Old Section
Luck	Ferdinand Ernest	1811-1882	Old Section

Calvary Cemetery Old and New Sections

Surname	First Name	Dates/Notes	Section
Luck	John W.	1867-1941	Old Section
Luck	Maggie E.	1870-1930	Old Section
Luck	Sarah F.	1899-1912	Old Section
Luck	William	1830-1915	Old Section
Lumpkins	Victoria Ida Mae	Mar 19, 1976 - Jan 4, 1995	Sect B
M	J	MJ handwritten, see J., M. died Jy 17, 1810	Old Section
Manning	Augusta	dau of W & M Manning, born Jan 23, 1854, died Aug 5, 1876	Old Section
Manning	Charity	wife of Nathan Manning, born Jun 1, 1782, died Jul 2, 1871, aged 89y 1m 1d, death date also states Jul 1st.	Old Section
Manning	George	son of WW & HA Manning, died Dec 30, 1863, aged 6y 7m (STONE MISSING)	Old Section
Manning	George G.	1838-1918	Sect A
Manning	Gerald R.	Jan 12, 1939 - Dec 24, 2003, wed Aug 1, 1959 to Marsail	Sect B
Manning	Josephine Irwin	wife of G.G. Manning, born Aug 17, 1855, died Mar 18, 1886	Old Section
Manning	Marsail	Nov 29, 1939 - Blank, wed Aug 1, 1959 to Gerald R. Manning	Sect B
Manning	Mary	wife of William S. Manning, born Jul 9, 1826, died Jul 27, 1907	Old Section
Manning	Mary Helen	1878-1954	Sect A
Manning	Nathan	born Sep 11, 1767, died Feb 23, 1858, aged 96 XX XX	Old Section
Manning	Oscar J.	son of J & M Manning, died at Camp Chase, O., Feb 11, 1865, aged 20y 2m 11d	Old Section
Manning	Rachel	wife of S. Manning, born Jan 28, 1812, died Aug 30, 1871	Old Section
Manning	Squire	born May 10, 1811, died Oct 18, 1889	Old Section
Manning	William S.	born Oct 2, 1818, died Jan 7, 1908	Old Section
Mappes	Henry	no dates	Sect B
Mappes	Katie	no dates	Sect B
Mappes	Mikle, Jr.	no dates	Sect B
Mappes	Mikle, Sr.	no dates	Sect B
Marsh	Mary	wife of Thomas L. Marsh, died Aug 1, 1855, age 76 year, 8 mos.	Old Section
Marsh	Thomas L.	died Aug 22, 1851, aged 78y 8m 2d	Old Section
Martis	Adophus M.	May 26, 1880 - Dec 6, 1956, wed Mar 23, 1929 to Callie Ruth Dunbar	Sect A
Martis	Callie Ruth Dunbar	Mar 23, 1901 - Apr 26, 1980, wed Mar 23, 1929 to Adophus M. Martis	Sect A
Martis	James Edward	Feb 16, 1886 - Oct 24, 1974	Sect A
Mathews	Hazel	1919-1974	Sect D
Mathews	Walter	1915-Blank	Sect D
Matthews	Mary F.	wife of Samuel G. Matthews, 1848-1909	Sect B
Matthews	Samuel G.	1833-1897	Sect B
May	Florence	1904-1990	Sect D
May	Glenn	1903-1963	Sect D
May	Harry L.	May 26, 1922 - Feb 25, 2007	Sect D
May	Harry Lee	PFC US Marine Corps, WWII, May 26, 1922 - Feb 25, 2007	Sect D

Calvary Cemetery Old and New Sections

Surname	Given Name	Details	Section
May	Rosella L. Boone	Jul 30, 1927 - Blank	Sect D
McCalla	Myrtle M.	1874-1942	Sect D
McCane	Claude T.	1905-1986	Sect C
McCane	Lela	1905-1966	Sect C
McCarter	Amelia	wife of Henry McCarter, died Dec 17, 1848 in 58th year	Old Section
McCarter	George W.	died Jun 2, 1846, aged 12y 6m 2d	Old Section
McCarter	Henry	died Apr 1, 1843, aged 57y 1m 28d	Old Section
McCarter	James H.	died Oct 17, 1843, aged 12y 8m 7d	Old Section
McCarter	Robert	died Oct 11, 1837, aged 17y 3m 23d	Old Section
McCullough	Emelyne Abrams	1893-1992, wife of John McCullough	Sect D
McCullough	Emma K.	1856-1932	Sect B
McCullough	Frances Whiteside	wife of Milton McCullough, 1916-2002	Sect D
McCullough	George F.	born in Mercer County, PA, Mar 17, 1818, died Mar 23, 1901	Sect B
McCullough	Georgie	son of WW & EC McCullough, born Sep 17, 1878, died Oct 25, 1880	Old Section
McCullough	John A.	1865-1937	Sect B
McCullough	John E.	1886-1972	Sect D
McCullough	Mary A.	dau of GF and Rachel McCullough, died Sep 18, 1860, aged 1y 11m	Old Section
McCullough	Milton W.	Tec 4 US Army, WWII, Aug 30, 1914 - Jun 17, 2002	Sect D
McCullough	Milton W., Dr.	Veteran, WWII, 1914-2002	Sect D
McCullough	Rachele	wife of George F. McCullough, born in Sangamon County, Ill, Nov 7, 1831, died Feb 18, 1909	Sect B
McCullough	Stanley	1881-1935	Sect B
McCullough	William W.	1854-1943	Sect B
McDulin	Charles	(Co. E 176 Ohio Inf). 1821 - 1883	Old Section
McDulin	Clara B.	1855-1916	Sect D
McDulin	Elizabeth	1826-1908	Old Section
McDulin	George W.	1849-1927	Sect D
McDulin	William	died Mar 10, 1890, aged 38y 9m 21d	Sect D
McKibben	Richard A.	Jul 6, 1957 - Feb 20, 2003	Sect D
McKibben	Roberta Helton	1918-1985	Sect D
McKinley	Benjamin	son of William and Jane McKinley, died Jul 25, 1834, aged 4y 6m 17d	Old Section
McKinley	Jane	wife of William McKinley, died Jul 24, 1834, aged 20y 7m 24d (STONE MISSING)	Old Section
McKinney	Isaac	died May 20, 1844, aged 25y 5m 3ds	Old Section
McKown	Christopher F.	son of J & C McKown, died Sep 13, 1848, aged 21y 6m 25 ds	Old Section
McMath	Anna E. Grimes	wife of Charles McMath, 1847-1907	Sect B
McMath	Charles	1847, Co. C 12 & 23 O. V. I. '61-'65, a prisoner of war 7 months	Sect B
McMath	Ethet G.	1869-19XX	Sect B
McMath	Mary K.	dau of Charles and Anna E. McMath, born Feb 5, 1876, died Mar 19, 1891	Sect B
McMullen	Edward	1878-1968	Sect D

Calvary Cemetery Old and New Sections

Surname	Given	Information	Section
McMullen	Florence A.	1886-1975	Sect D
McWilliams	Joseph	son of John and Nancy McWilliams, died Jan 10, 1836 in 20th year(STONE MISSING)	Old Section
McWilliams	Nancy	wife of John McWilliams, died Aug 3, 1834 in 56th year	Old Section
Means	Anna Kay	Oct 11, 1961 - Aug 5, 2003	Sect C
Mears	Alice	1868-1962	Old Section
Mears	John J.	1838-1919	Old Section
Mears	Josephine	1844-1917	Old Section
Meek	John, Rev.	born in Virginia, Jul 7, 1781, died Dec 30, 1860	Old Section
Meek	Martha	died Sep 23, 1868, aged 87y 2m	Old Section
Melvin	Bobby	Dec 28, 1930 - Nov 16, 2009, wed Nov 2, 1951 to Eleanor	Sect C
Melvin	Eleanor	Apr 17, 1930 - Apr 25, 2001, wed Nov 2, 1951 to Bobby Melvin	Sect C
Meranda	Beulah L.	1885-1966	Sect D
Meranda	Doris E.	Sep 16, 1921 - Dec 29, 2001	Sect C
Meranda	Infant son	1936 - son of Ruth J. Meranda	Sect D
Meranda	Joseph S.	1885-1941	Sect D
Meranda	Paul David	Dec 13, 1920 - May 23, 1991	Sect C
Meranda	Paul David	1st Sgt US Army, WWII, Co H 95 Division 379th Infantry, Dec 13, 1920 - May 23, 1991	Sect C
Meranda	Ruth J.	1916-1936	Sect D
Metz	Elizabeth	wife of T. J. Metz, 1832-1916	Sect A
Metz	T. J.	1836-1913	Sect A
Metzger	Catherine J. B.	wife of George Metzger, born Oct 26, 1847, died Jan 19, 1897	Sect B
Metzger	George	born Nov 4, 1843, died Dec 24, 1904	Sect B
Meyers	June	1921-1969	Sect A
Meyers	Raymond	1903-1974	Sect A
Miller	Allen W.	1839-1904	Sect D
Miller	Curt	L. Curtis Miller, born Jul 21, 1864, died Jun 14, 1943 son of Lewis and Margaret F. Miller, died in Kenton County, KY.	Sect D
Miller	Edgar W.	son of AW and ME Miller, 1881-1907	Sect D
Miller	Elizabeth	wife of Thomas Miller, died Jun 19, 1870, in 70th year of her age	Old Section
Miller	Elmer M.	Nov 19, 1922 - May 13, 1999	Sect D
Miller	Elmer Milton	US Army, WWII, Nov 19, 1922 - May 13, 1999	Sect D
Miller	Lewis L.	1829-1908	Sect D
Miller	Margaret E.	1837-1917	Sect D
Miller	Maria E.	1843-1926	Sect D
Miller	Mary L. Corbin	Dec 8, 1925 - Sep 5, 2006	Sect D
Miller	Thomas	born 1803, died Sep 4, 1849, aged 46 years	Old Section
Minzler	Bernard	Dec 19, 1930 - Sep 13, 1991	Sect A

Calvary Cemetery Old and New Sections

Surname	First Name	Dates / Notes	Section
Minzler	Carl J.	1932-2002	Sect A
Minzler	Mary F.	1922-1991	Sect A
Mitchell	Clyde E.	1906-1978	Sect D
Mitchell	Ina M.	1902-1961	Sect D
Mitchell	Layrue	Dec 31, 1937 - Mar 21, 2009	Sect C
Mitchell	Lowell T.	Nov 24, 1930 - Aug 9, 2004	Sect D
Mitchell	Ruth	Aug 11, 1940 - Blank	Sect C
Molen	Joseph P.	born Oct 12, 1813, died Dec 12, 1870	Old Section
Molen	Martha Warden	wife of Joseph P. Molen, born Feb 24, 1823, died Aug 19, 1894	Old Section
Moore	Carey Runyon	Tec4 US Army WWII, Oct 2, 1917 - Feb 27, 1980	Sect A
Moore	Ella F.	Oct 29, 1925 - Apr 28, 2008	Sect A
Moore	J. L., MD	born Oct 17, 1851, died Oct 21, 1885	Sect B
Moore	Larry T.	Nov 2, 1946 - Blank	Sect A
Moreton	David B.	1845-1923	Sect B
Moreton	Julia Hawk	1878-1957	Sect B
Moreton	Louise J.	1896-1954	Sect B
Moreton	Louise Pattison	wife of David Moreton, 1853-1925	Sect B
Moreton	William Clifford	1876-1908	Sect B
Morgan	Archie, Jr.	Jul 17, 1940 - Blank, wed Oct 4, 1966 to Norma Jean Oney	Sect B
Morgan	Norma Jean Oney	Jun 25, 1946 - Mar 23, 2008, wed Oct 4, 1966 to Archie Morgan, Jr.	Sect B
Morlatt	Floyd D.	son of Jean and Kenneth Morlatt, Jul 8, 1952 - Dec 28, 1973	Sect C
Morlatt	Jackie	Jul 29, 1967 - Nov 18, 1973	Sect C
Morlatt	Jean Gorth	Jun 11, 1926 - Jun 17, 2007	Sect C
Morlatt	Kenda	May 31, 1969 - Nov 18, 1973	Sect C
Morlatt	Kenneth N.	PFC US Army, WWII, Aug 28, 1927 - May 19, 1989	Sect C
Morlatt	Kenneth N.	Aug 28, 1927 - May 19, 1989	Sect C
Morlatt	Neal G.	Aug 1, 1950 - Oct 13, 1994	Sect C
Morlatt	Walter J.	son of Jean and Kenneth Morlatt, Jul 2, 1958 - Apr 14, 1973	Sect C
Moyer	Daniel	1824-1912	Sect A
Moyer	Elizabeth	1841-1929	Sect B
Moyer	Hannah Carter	1837-1918	Sect A
Moyer	Hester A.	dau of J & S Moyer, died Feb 18, 1855, aged 16y 2m 20d	Old Section
Moyer	Infant dau	of J & S Moyer erected 1856	Old Section
Moyer	Melancton	member of Co. B. 59 Reg. O. V. I. at Nashville, Tenn, Sep 17, 1864, aged 21y 3m 3d	Old Section
Moyer	Thomas J.	1841-1915, Co K 145 OVI	Sect B
Muncy	J. B.	Blank	Sect A
Muncy	James	1902-1977	Sect A
Muncy	James B.	Jul 19, 1934 - Jun 26, 1998	Sect A

Calvary Cemetery Old and New Sections

Surname	Given Name	Details	Section
Muncy	Laura	1901-1998	Sect A
Muncy	Marietta	Oct 26, 1940 - Blank	Sect A
Musser	Robert D.	Mar 14, 1900 - Oct 30, 1971	Sect B
Napier	Celia J. Theademan	Aug 11, 1938 - Aug 22, 2004, wed Aug 6, 1955 to Hamblin Napier	Sect C
Napier	Charlie	Sep 15, 1942 - Sep 28, 1995	Sect C
Napier	Ella M. Terry	Jul 9, 1940 - May 17, 2004	Sect C
Napier	Hamblin	PFC US Army, Korea, Jan 14, 1927 - Apr 14, 2003	Sect C
Napier	Hamblin	Jan 14, 1927 - Apr 14, 2003, wed Aug 6, 1955 to Celia J. Theademan	Sect C
Napier	John H.	Aug 18, 1964 - Sep 11, 1999	Sect C
Napier	Malissia E. Gray	Jan 20, 1952 - Sep 29, 2010	Sect C
Napier	Mark D.	Dec 28, 1967 - Jul 25, 2001	Sect C
Napier	Roger W.	1960-1977	Sect C
Neal	Charles E., Sr.	May 21, 1937 - May 8, 2009	Sect C
Neal	Geraldine	Jan 31, 1939 - Sep 17, 2008	Sect C
Neftzer	Archie Lee	Ohio PVT 1 Gas Regt. WW1, born Mar 21, 1897, died Jul 15, 1946	Sect B
Neftzer	Charles F.	1880-1903	Sect D
Neftzer	Edna Z. Behymer	May 9, 1900- Aug 27, 1983	Sect B
Neftzer	Frank William	Sep 8, 1868 - Oct 15, 1906	Sect A
Neftzer	George	1854-1923	Sect D
Neftzer	Gus William	Gus, 1883-1902	Sect D
Neftzer	Harley LeRoy	Aug 5, 1937 - Jul 28, 1998, wed May 19, 1958 to Ruby Lee	Sect B
Neftzer	Jacob F.	1825-1892	Sect A
Neftzer	John	Apr 16, 1856 - Aug 24, 1901, aged 45y 4m 8ds	Sect A
Neftzer	John Jacob	born Jul 25, 1866, died Apr 7, 1900	Sect A
Neftzer	Joseph Alen	Feb 14, 1967 - Aug 20, 2001	Sect B
Neftzer	Kenneth R., Sr.	May 7, 1935- Blank, wed Nov 12, 1954 to Ruth M. Welch, USAF	Sect A
Neftzer	Loaf	Feb 16, 1858 - Apr 15, 1905, aged 47y 1m 20d	Sect A
Neftzer	Mary	wife of George Neftzer, 1863-1927	Sect D
Neftzer	Mary E. Ritter	May 1, 1936 - Blank	Sect B
Neftzer	Michael Anthony	May 3, 1964 - May 3, 1964	Sect B
Neftzer	Orville E.	Jul 29, 1920 - Dec 17, 1922	Sect B
Neftzer	Ralph W.	Jun 12, 1927 - Mar 22, 1929	Sect B
Neftzer	Rosa	1831-1889	Sect A
Neftzer	Roy E.	May 22, 1924 - Mar 16, 1994	Sect B
Neftzer	Ruby Lee	Nov 18, 1936 - Blank, wed May 19, 1958 to Harley Leroy Neftzer	Sect B
Neftzer	Ruth M. Welch	Sep 28, 1935 - Blank, wed Nov 12, 1954 to Kenneth R. Neftzer, Sr.	Sect A
Neftzer	Samuel D.	born Jun 11, 1871, died Feb 25, 1898	Sect A
Neftzer	Vernon A.	Sep 28, 1922 - Aug 4, 1944	Sect B

Calvary Cemetery Old and New Sections

Surname	Given Name	Details	Section
Neiman	Harry G.	no dates	Sect B
Neiman	Louise	wife of Harry G. Neiman, no dates	Sect B
Newport	Jeremy J.	Nov 10, 1992 - Jun 23, 2001, grandson of Ruth & Layrue Mitchell	Sect C
Nichols	Albert W.	son of JS & Mary L. Nichols, died Mar 16, 1878, aged 13y 3m 11d	Old Section
Nichols	Flora	born Sep 1, 1862, died Dec 19, 1885	Old Section
Nichols	James T.	died Apr 17, 1878, aged 41y 5m 17d	Old Section
Nichols	John S.	died Feb 13, 1878, aged 44y 8m 24d	Old Section
Nichols	Lizzie M.	dau of Thomas J & C Nichols, died May 3, 1878, aged 18y 5m 6d	Old Section
Nichols	Mary L.	died Mar 6, 1916, aged 74y 8m 12d	Old Section
Nichols	Missouri E.	born Jan 31, 1838, died Nov 30, 1886	Old Section
Nichols	T. J.	born Mar 18, 1831, died Jan 18, 1898	Old Section
Nichols	Virginia A.	wife of Thomas J. Nichols, died Apr 22, 1883, aged 51y 4m 19ds	Old Section
Nichols	William W.	born Jan 3, 1858, died Jun 5, 1887	Old Section
Nichols	Willie	son of JA and AM Nichols, died Aug 1, 1875, aged 6m 20d	Old Section
Nickol	Damian Zane	son of Rachel Nickol, Nov 13, 2000 - Nov 16, 2000	Sect C
Noble	Granville Brian, Jr.	son of Granville Brian and Tammy Sue Noble, Mar 8, 1996 - Jul 29, 1996	Sect C
Norris	Ella	1853-1944	Sect D
Norris	George F.	born Aug 12, 1874, died Oct 18, 1882 (STONE MISSING)	Old Section
Norris	Harrison	born Oct 20, 1813, died Jan 29, 1868	Old Section
Norris	Jane	wife of Harrison Norris, born Jan 3, 1816, died Oct 9, 1888	Old Section
Norris	Johnie H.	son of William and Eliza Norris, died Aug 7, 1864, aged 1y 7m 18d	Old Section
Norris	Robert	1846-1935	Sect D
Norris	William	died Nov 23, 1870 in 53rd year of his age	Old Section
Nort	Catherine Miller	wife of Jacob Nort, born Jan 31, 1826, died Jul 21, 1892, aged 66y 6m 21ds	Sect D
Nort	Jacob	born Mar 2, 1820, died Mar 12, 1899, aged 79 yrs 10 ds	Sect D
Oliver	Harvey L.	Jul 28, 1920 - Mar 13, 2009	Sect A
Oliver	Maebelle	May 30, 1940 - Mar 15, 1989	Sect A
Oney	Bertha Mae Gibson	Feb 24, 1914 - Feb 15, 1991	Sect B
Oney	Earl Haskel	Dec 15, 1912 - Jul 5, 2002	Sect B
Oney	Melinda Ellen	Sep 10, 1974 - Mar 15, 1993	Sect B
Orme	Lindsey N.	1989-2011	Sect D
Padget	Ada Liza	dau of William and Matilda A. Padgett, born Mar 29, 1848, died Jun 6, 1851	Old Section
Padget	Emma	dau of William & Matilda A. Padgett, died Apr 14, 1858, aged 8m 29d	Old Section
Padget	Freddie M.	son of TL and HA Padget, born Apr 20, 1884, died Oct 23, 1890	Sect B
Padget	Hercilia A.	wife of T. L. Padget, born Sep 8, 1841, died Oct 9, 1900	Sect B
Padget	John L.	Jun 4, 1842 - Feb 22, 1922	Old Section
Padget	Lowell	son of JT & HE Padgett, born Mar 8, 1880, died Nov 20, 1882	Old Section
Padget	Matilda A.	wife of William, died Sep 10, 1877, aged 63y 9m 28d	Old Section

28

Calvary Cemetery Old and New Sections

Surname	Given Name	Details	Section
Padget	Sarah C.	wife of John L., Apr 25, 1848 - Jan 2, 1928	Old Section
Padget	Thomas L.	born Nov 12, 1838, died Aug 25, 1903	Sect B
Padget	William	died Apr 5, 1885, aged 72y 4m 16d	Old Section
Padget	William B. C.	son of William and Matilda A. Padgett, died May 19, 1861, aged 21y 1m 20d	Old Section
Padget	William R.	(stone missing) son of TL and HA Padgett, born Mar 17, 1878, died Mar 23, 1888	Sect B
Padget	Willie M.	son of JL and C Padget, born Oct 1, 1875, died Nov 1, 1881	Old Section
Page	Benjamin F.	son of MC & SC Page, died Oct 24, 1844, aged 4ms 5ds	Old Section
Page	Emma N.	dau of TW & EJ Page, died Nov 16, 1864, aged 16y 7m 2d	Old Section
Page	Joseph	died May 17, 1867, aged 66y 1m 3d	Old Section
Page	Mollie C.	dau of Rev. William P. and M. Page, died Oct 22, 1876, aged 67y 1m 3d	Old Section
Page	Molly	consort of Rev. William Page, May 7, 1815, in 41st year	Old Section
Page	Molly	wife of of William Page, died May 7, 1815 - in 40th year	Old Section
Page	Nancy B.	wife of Joseph Page, died Feb 18, 1873 in 68th year	Old Section
Page	William, Rev.	died Nov 15, 1834 - 63 years	Old Section
Page	William, Rev.	died Nov 15, 1834 aged 62y (2nd stone)	Old Section
Pangburn	Clarence E.	1882-1957	Sect D
Pangburn	Georgia A.	1881-1954	Sect D
Pangburn	Ida	1857-1936	Sect D
Pangburn	William J.	1859-1935	Sect D
Parker	Dewey H.	Apr 17, 1902 - Apr 25, 1979	Sect B
Parker	Myles E. "Pete"	SP4 US Army Korea, Vietnam, Oct 15, 1934 - Apr 8, 2004	Sect B
Patison	N	1822	Old Section
Patterson	Oletha J.	wife of JH Patterson, died Jan 15, 1879, aged 27y 4d	Old Section
Pattison	Anna	1868-1941	Sect B
Pattison	Cinda A.	1826-1917	Sect B
Pattison	George R.	1863-1936	Sect B
Pattison	Henry C.	1858-1935	Sect B
Pattison	Lydia H.	1861-1917	Sect B
Pattison	W. G.	1819-1915	Sect B
Pattison	W. Quincy	1865-1966	Sect B
Pauly	Gladys C.	Apr 30, 1927 - Apr 14, 1976	Sect A
Pauly	Louis, Jr.	PVT US Army, Korea, Nov 20, 1929 - Feb 20, 2002	Sect A
Pauly	William E.	Oct 8, 1955 - Jan 29, 1979	Sect A
Peirce	Anna	1841 - 1887	Sect B
Penn	Caroline	wife of Elijah T. Penn, died Jul 11, 1864, aged 53 years	Old Section
Penn	Elijah T.	died Sep 15, 1877, aged 84y 8m 18d	Old Section
Penn	Elizabeth C. Sargent	wife of Elijah T. Penn, died Jan 10, 1870 in 64th year of age	Old Section
Penn	George W.	died Jan 21, 1863, aged 25y 6m 21d	Old Section

Calvary Cemetery Old and New Sections

Surname	Given Name	Details	Section
Penn	John F. William	son of William and Elizabeth Penn, died Sep 18, 1844, aged 6m 13d	Old Section
Penn	Maggie B.	dau of JW & NV Penn, died Feb 24, 1866, aged 2y 7m 3d	Old Section
Penn	Mary Ellen	dau of Elijah T and Philenia Penn, born Jul 13, 1821, died Feb 1. 1852	Old Section
Penn	Maryann Rebecca	born Oct 9, 1811, died Apr 2, 1833	Old Section
Penn	Milton T.	son of JW and NV Penn, died Jan 29, 1866, aged 4y 8m 27d	Old Section
Penn	Philenia W.	wife of ET Penn, died Apr 12, 1849, aged 51y 11m 23d	Old Section
Penn	Rebecca	wife of Joseph W. Penn, died Apr 22, 1856, aged 21y 4m 12d	Old Section
Penn	Sallie L.	dau of George W. and Maggie Penn, died Jan 17, 1868, aged 7y 5m	Old Section
Penn	William	born Mar 14, 1803, died Jan 4, 1844	Old Section
Pennington	Brad	US Marine Corps, Dec 28, 1960 - Mar 27, 2006	Sect C
Pennington	Brad	Dec 28, 1960 - Mar 27, 2006	Sect C
Pennington	Elizabeth	1916-Blank	Sect D
Pennington	Ray	1908-1975	Sect D
Peters	Addie Mae	Nov 24, 1923 - Aug 27, 2004	Sect A
Peters	E. Earl	Apr 22, 1913 - Jun 7, 1987	Sect A
Pfifer	David	mem of Co. D., 7 Regt. O.V.C., died May 31, 1864, 28 years	Old Section
Phillips	Alexander	died Oct 16, 1859 - 66 years old	Old Section
Phillips	Alexander W.	born Dec 19, 1837, died Aug 30, 1862	Old Section
Phillips	Andrew	died 1851, aged 50 years	Old Section
Phillips	Charles E.	1898-1965	Sect D
Phillips	Charles G.	CPL US Marine Corp WWII, Co. A. 1st BN 4th Marines, 6th Marine Division, Jan 9, 1926 - Sep 21, 2002	Sect C
Phillips	Charles G.	Jan 9. 1926 - Sep 21, 2002	Sect C
Phillips	Edna L.	1899-1972	Sect D
Phillips	Elizabeth Helen Gregg	wife of F. J. Phillips, died Sep 21, 1849 in 26th year of her life (Buchanan lot)	Old Section
Phillips	Elvira	dau of Alexander and Mary Phillips, Nov 13, 1833, aged 10y 1m 24d	Old Section
Phillips	F. J.	1815-1881	Old Section
Phillips	G.G.	1888-1888	Old Section
Phillips	George G.	1862-1941	Sect D
Phillips	Infant daughter	Jan 18, 1897	Sect D
Phillips	Marguerite L. Gates	Apr 15, 1924 - Blank	Sect C
Phillips	Martha	died May 25, 1859 - 54y 4m 24d	Old Section
Phillips	Martha	wife of Thomas Phillips, died Sep 21, 1843, aged 76 years	Old Section
Phillips	Mary	wife of Alexander Phillips, born Aug 10, 1795, died Jan 7, 1851, aged 75y 4m 27ds	Old Section
Phillips	Mary L.	1866-1942	Sect D
Phillips	Sarah E.	1865-1908	Old Section
Phillips	Thomas	died Oct 28, 1854, aged 88 years	Old Section

30

Calvary Cemetery Old and New Sections

Surname	Given Name	Details	Section
Philpot	Maxine	Dec 14, 1928 - Oct 1, 1991	Sect D
Pierce	Edna May	1915-2008	Sect D
Pierce	Robert L.	1915-1969	Sect D
Pike	Blanche	1911-1963	Sect B
Pike	Charles	Mar 20, 1930 - Jul 29, 1978	Sect B
Pike	Nadine	Oct 28, 1929 - Dec 5, 1996	Sect D
Pingle	Christina	wife of John G. Pingle, 1867-1918	Sect D
Pingle	John G.	1868-1951	Sect D
Pingle	John Louis	1896-1934	Sect D
Pitzer	Lillian Wilson	Oct 17, 1912 - May 12, 2003	Old Section
Plackard	Charlotte M.	wife of TL Planchard, born Jan 27, 1834, died Sep 12, 1872	Old Section
Plackard	Fee	son of V & J Plackard, born May 5, 1871, died Feb 12, 1875	Old Section
Plackard	Jacob	born Dec 25, 1807, died Sep 20, 1880	Old Section
Plackard	Leanor	wife of Jacob Plackard, born Dec 29, 1813, died Aug 15, 1898	Old Section
Planck	Mary M.	wife of Michael Planck, died Sep 18, 1877, aged 79y 8m 31d	Old Section
Poe	James K.	died Jul 3, 1865 in 22nd year	Sect A
Poe	Joshua Wayne	May 5, 1995 - Oct 11, 1996	Sect B
Poe	Ruth A.	Aug 16, 1927 - May 12, 2009	Old Section
Poe	Sarah	born Nov 19, 1799, died Feb 20, 1880	Sect B
Poe	Thomas H.	Mar 15, 1919 - Dec 11, 1979	Sect A
Pollock	Patricia L. Collins	Feb 19, 1937 - Sep 9, 1990	Sect B
Porste	Emma E.	Aug 4, 1888 - Nov 17, 1977	Sect B
Porste	James	Jan 3, 1860 - Jun 24, 1906	Sect B
Porste	William	son of Willmina and James Porste, Nov 5, 1891 - Jul 2, 1908	Sect B
Porste	Willmina	wife of James Porste, Feb 15, 1870 - Nov 23, 1946	Old Section
Powell	Elmira J.	dau of Joseph L. & Juliet Powell, died Feb 9, 1847, aged 10m 6d	Old Section
Powell	Juliet	consort of Joseph L. Powell, died Dec 31, 1846, aged 28y 9m 16d	Old Section
Preston	Elbert, Sr.	Mar 21, 1929 - Blank, wed Jul 7, 1950 to Sylvia	Sect C
Preston	Sylvia	Jul 12, 1930 - Mar 26, 2002, wed Jul 7, 1950 to Elbert Preston, Sr.	Sect C
Preuer	Albert	1870-1922	Sect A
Preuer	Susie	1866-1931	Sect A
Pribble	Jennie	1859-1944	Sect B
Purkhiser	Catherine	wife of Michael Purkhiser, died Jan 6, 1833, aged 82	Old Section
Purkhiser	Eliza Rebecca	wife of Lorenzo Dow Purkhiser, born Sep 17, 1816, died Oct 23, 1891, 75y 1, 6ds	Sect C
Purkhiser	Elizabeth	wife of Henry Purkhiser, died Aug 30, 1822, aged 29y 5m 17d	Old Section
Purkhiser	Harry F.	son of MH & SA Purkhiser, born June 6, 1878, died Mar 15, 1881	Old Section
Purkhiser	Henry	died Dec 21, 1840, aged 54y 2m 7d	Old Section
Purkhiser	Howard H.	son of MH & SA Purkhiser, died Aug 27, 1884, aged 1y 4m 27d	Old Section

Calvary Cemetery Old and New Sections

Surname	Given Name	Details	Section
Purkhiser	Infant Son	of JS & SL Purkhiser, died Feb 12, 1842	Old Section
Purkhiser	John S.	died Jan 14, 1900, aged 80y 8 m 15d	Old Section
Purkhiser	Lorenza	son, died Jun 4, 1880, aged 21y 3m 16d	Sect C
Purkhiser	Lorenzo Dow	born Jun 16, 1815, died Oct 14, 1887, aged 72y 3m 23ds	Sect C
Purkhiser	Mary Dow	born Jan 4, 1848, died Jun 21, 1851	Old Section
Purkhiser	Mary Elizabeth	dau died Feb 1, 1857, aged 1y 8m 3d	Old Section
Purkhiser	Michael	died Oct 31, 1816, aged 80 years	Old Section
Purkhiser	Michael Henry	son of JS & SL Purkhiser, died Mar 1, 1845, aged 3m 19d	Old Section
Purkhiser	Peggy	died Aug 17, 1862, aged 78 years	Old Section
Purkhiser	Sarah Caroline	born Jul 3, 1845, died Feb 18, 1850	Sect C
Purkhiser	Sarah L.	wife of John S. Purkhiser, died Nov 29, 1889, aged 62y 11m 28d	Old Section
Purkiser	Charles Augustus	son of William P. and Eliza, died Jul 12, 1859, 9m 18d	Old Section
Purkiser	Fanny	wife of Marcus H. Purkiser, died Aug 12, 1845, aged 42y 4m 12d	Old Section
Purkiser	George W.	1 Ohio L. A.	Sect A
Purkiser	John R.	son of MH and F Purkiser, died Apr 18, 1839, aged 13y 7m 23d	Old Section
Purkiser	Jonathan G.	son of MH & F Purkiser, died Oct 15, 1855, aged 14y 8m 11d	Old Section
Purkiser	Leroy S.	died Aug 29, 1854, aged 32y 11, 1d	Old Section
Purkiser	M	MP footstone	Old Section
Purkiser	M.H.	died May 16, 1870 in 71st year	Old Section
Purkiser	Marcus H.	son of MH & F Purkiser, died Jul 27, 1838, aged 4y10m27d	Old Section
Purkiser	Michael	died Jun 19, 1852, aged 66y 3m 4d	Old Section
Purkiser	Rachel	wife of Marcus Purkiser, died Jul 10, 1851, aged 38y 9m 14ds	Old Section
Purkiser	Sarah C.	dau of LD and ER Purkiser, died Feb 18, 1850, aged 4y 7m 15d	Old Section
Pursley	Charlene Holland	Jan 26, 1966 - Nov 13, 1995	Sect C
Rardon	Robert Harrison	died Nov 28, 1874, aged 7y 5m 4d	Old Section
Reichard	Ruth L.	Mar 10, 1906 - Jan 7, 1998	Sect A
Reynolds	Carolyn M.	Jan 30, 1944 - Blank, wed Jan 9, 1963 to Vernon Freeman Reynolds	Sect C
Reynolds	Florence Bays	Aug 10, 1901 - Oct 4, 1995, wed May 29, 1930 to Freeman Reynolds	Sect C
Reynolds	Freeman	Jan 21, 1902 - Oct 3, 1980, wed May 29, 1930 to Florence Bays	Sect C
Reynolds	James Freeman	Feb 22, 1984- Aug 28, 2000	Sect C
Reynolds	Vernon Freeman	Jan 9, 1944 - Feb 28, 2007, wed Jan 9, 1963 to Carolyn M.	Sect C
Richards	Anastasia	Aug 21, 1852 - Jan 12, 1938	Old Section
Richards	Ann	wife of George Richards, born Apr 11, 1778, died Aug 3, 1849	Old Section
Richards	Bena Smith	wife of Robert J. Richards, born Jul 7, 1822, died Mar 17, 1898	Old Section
Richards	Brett Thomas	Sep 5, 1977 - May 11, 2002	Sect C
Richards	Charles F.	son of Robert and Bena Richards, born Aug 21, 1852, died Dec 30, 1854	Old Section
Richards	Charlie	son of William F. and Rosanna Richards, died Dec 26, 1862	Old Section

Calvary Cemetery Old and New Sections

Surname	Given Name	Details	Section
Richards	Ethel Marie	(stone missing) dau of Frank and Grace Richards, died Mar 6, 1894	Sect B
Richards	Ezra	son of John and Ann Richards, died Jul 10, 1822, aged 2m 15d	Old Section
Richards	George	died Jun 2, 1848, aged 77y 2m	Old Section
Richards	George W.	born Nov 12, 1849, died Mar 6, 1934	Old Section
Richards	Harriet E.	dau of John and Ann Richards, died Dec 3, 1846, aged 22y 5m 3d	Old Section
Richards	Jane	consort of Samuel Richards, died Apr 5, 1837, aged 32 yrs	Old Section
Richards	Jerusha E.	died Apr 17, 1855 in 20th year of age	Old Section
Richards	Jessie R.	born Feb 27, 1874 - 1948	Old Section
Richards	John	died Aug 3, 1849, aged 61y 6m 2d	Old Section
Richards	John G.	died Jun 8, 1872, aged 61y 14d	Old Section
Richards	Mary	consort of Noah Richards, died Jun 1, 1845, aged 46y 9m 25d	Old Section
Richards	Mary Ann	dau of N & Mary Richards, died Feb 3, 1854 in 14th year	Old Section
Richards	Mary E.	wife of GW Richards, born Mar 2, 1849, died Oct 28, 1898	Old Section
Richards	Nackey E.	wife of R. B. Richards, 1834-1919	Old Section
Richards	Nancy B.	wife of John G. Richards, died Jul 28, 1866, aged 45y 1m 3d	Old Section
Richards	Nannie E.	dau of GW and ME Richards, born May 10, 1870, died Mar 6, 1883	Old Section
Richards	Noah	died Jun 4, 1866, aged 68y 5m 11d	Old Section
Richards	R. B.	1827-1908	Old Section
Richards	Robert J.	born Aug 11, 1825, died Aug 5, 1909	Old Section
Richards	Thomas S.	son of John and Ann Richards, born Dec 18, 1837, died Oct 5, 1868	Old Section
Riggin	Sarah	born in Nicholas Co., Ky, died at Pt, Isabel, Ohio, Aug 25, 1881, aged 83 years	Old Section
Ritchie	Thresa Louise	Nov 2, 1952 - Jul 3, 1998	Sect C
Robbins	Stephen	died Aug 4, 1845, 92 years	Old Section
Robinson	Deloris	Jan 18, 1919- Aug 31, 2000	Sect B
Robinson	Theoflas	Jun 14, 1907 - Oct 6, 1980	Sect B
Rogers	Deborah	wife of Reuben Rogers, died Jul 19, 1861, aged 57y 9m 13d	Old Section
Rogg	Charles	1946-2005 with Hazel M. Hiles	Sect C
Rouse	Mary Ann	wife of MG Rouse, born Mar 11, 1840, died Jul 19, 1890	Sect B
Rudd	Brady Jay	Jul 8, 1980 - Dec 20, 1997	Sect B
Rudd	Edgar	Jun 15, 1909 - Jun 27, 1998, wed Jul 19, 1930 to Nora Lee Arnett	Sect B
Rudd	Nora Lee Arnett	Oct 11, 1913 - May 4, 2010, wed Jul 19, 1930 to Edgar Rudd	Sect B
Rush	Leeana	dau of RD and SE Rush, died Jul 16, 1854, aged 1y 5m 14d (STONE MISSING)	Old Section
Rush	Sarah	wife of Richard Rush, died May 17, 1859 or 1853, aged 31y 8m 17d	Old Section
Russell	Forest E.	Mar 3, 1919 - Jul 26, 1998	Sect D
Russell	Richard W.	Nov 9, 1927 - Jan 27, 1990	Sect C
Rust	Charles P.	only son of Paul E. & Elizabeth M. Rust, born Aug 23, 1848, died Sep 11, 1873	Sect A
Rust	Elizabeth Margaret	wife of P. E. Rust, Jun 8, 1826 - Jun 26, 1903	Sect A
Rust	Florence	dau of Paul and Elizabeth M. Rust, Jun 7, 1867 - Jun 30, 1915	Sect A

Calvary Cemetery Old and New Sections

Surname	Given Name	Details	Section
Rust	Ida	dau of Paul E. and Elizabeth M. Rust, Aug 2, 1853 - Feb 17, 1855	Sect A
Rust	Nette	born Aug 2, 1860, died Dec 11, 1927	Sect A
Rust	Paul Eldridge	born Sep 5, 1823, died Feb 21, 1891	Sect A
Salt	Clemma Day	1858-1938	Sect B
Salt	Edward W.	1860-1934	Sect B
Salt	Grace G.	1897-1992	Sect B
Salt	John	died Oct 9, 1859, aged 76y 1m 29d	Old Section
Salt	Maggie T.	born Mar 20, 1860, died May 1, 1895	Sect B
Salt	Nancy	wife of John Salt died Jan 5, 1845, aged 56y 11m 1d. (ON VERY LARGE FLAT STONE) Mrs Salt was a dau of Daniel and Elizabeth Donavan b. in Haverdegrass, MD 1789 moved to Bracken Co., KY 1792 married John Salt in 1809 moved to Clermont Co., OH, died in 1845.	Old Section
Salt	Ray G.	1888-1975	Sect B
Sapp	Hartily	died Apr 29, 1840, aged 53y 3m 7d	Old Section
Sapp	Mary	wife of H. Sapp, died Oct 15, 1850, aged 55y 8m 8d (STONE MISSING)	Old Section
Sargent	Addie E.	1853-1934	Sect D
Sargent	Addie J.	Dec 29, 1897 - Nov 28, 1974	Sect D
Sargent	C. W.	1847-1926	Sect D
Sargent	Doris A. Garrison	Apr 26, 1937 - Jan 24, 1988	Sect D
Sargent	Esther Ann	dau of Joseph Sargent, died Apr 29, 1880	Old Section
Sargent	George G.	1846-1933	Old Section
Sargent	Infant Daughter	Dec 8, 1924, dau of Joseph and Addie Sargent	Sect D
Sargent	James A.	1811-1882	Old Section
Sargent	Joseph T.	CPL US Army, WWI, 1897 - 1979	Sect D
Sargent	Kenneth Smith	son of Joseph and Addie Sargent, Aug 28, 1923	Sect D
Sargent	Mary E.	1818-1890	Old Section
Schmidt	Charles	1826-1910	Sect D
Schmidt	Charles P.	1868-1936	Sect D
Schmidt	Henry	1870-1901	Sect D
Schmidt	John	1859-1901	Sect D
Schmidt	Katherine	wife of Charles Schmidt, 1834-1910	Sect D
Schmidt	William J.	1864-1911	Sect D
Schwab	Carrie I.	Apr 25, 1899 - Dec 16, 1977	Sect D
Schwab	Charles K.	1860-1915	Sect D
Schwab	Etha Shinkle	Apr 16, 1915 - Jan 1, 1996	Sect C
Schwab	James L.	May 24, 1917 - Nov 18, 1978	Sect C
Schwab	James R.	Apr 10, 1940 - Sep 27, 1979	Sect C

Calvary Cemetery Old and New Sections

Last Name	First Name	Details	Section
Schwab	James Robert	PFC US Army, 1940 - 1979	Sect C
Schwab	John, Jr.	1854-1913	Sect D
Schwab	John, Sr.	born in Baden, Germany Jul 8, 1820, died Jun 5,1896	Sect D
Schwab	Margaret Decker	wife of John Schwab, Sr. born Aug 10, 1824, died Jul 15, 1905	Sect D
Schwab	Marjorie L.	Sep 24, 1932 - Blank	Sect C
Schwab	Mary L.	wife of John Schwab, Jr. 1858-1940	Sect D
Schwab	Mother and Sister	no dates	Sect D
Scott	Emma	Apr 13, 1930 - Blank, wed Oct 26, 1946 to Lloyd G. Scott	Sect A
Scott	John	died Jun 6, 1844 in 59th year	Old Section
Scott	Lloyd G.	Dec 13, 1927 - Nov 21, 1995, wed Oct 26, 1946 to Emma	Sect A
Scott	Michael Dean	Feb 28, 1954 - Dec 29, 1975	Sect A
Seiger	Dorothy M. Luck	Sep 3, 1926 - Jan 20, 2010	Sect C
Seiger	E. Bruce	Jan 25, 1922 - Aug 13, 1997	Sect C
Seiger	E. Bruce	T SGT US Army WWII, Jan 25, 1922 - Aug 13, 1997	Sect C
Setz	Samuel	born Sep 25, 1842, died Aug 20, 1876	Old Section
Seymore	Mary E.	1855-1892	Sect B
Shafer	Leona F. Leach	Aug 4, 1918 - Jul 30, 1983	Sect D
Shamblin	Chester	Dec 9, 1907 - May 29, 1992	Sect B
Shamblin	Kenneth Ray	A3C US Air Force, May 12, 1935 - Jan 11, 1997	Sect B
Shelley	Pamela Mineer	Nov 1, 1956 - Jun 14, 2006	Sect D
Shinkle	Bernice M.	May 18, 1904 - Aug 16, 1985	Sect C
Shinkle	Cassius S.	1871-1950	Sect C
Shinkle	Elizabeth	1869-1921	Sect C
Short	Neal B., Jr.	Dec 21, 1949 - May 5, 2001	Sect C
Short	Robert J.	son of Cathy Mannino, Sep 16, 1990 - Oct 14, 1990	Sect A
Shrum	Arthur B.	1900-1975	Sect C
Shrum	Louise	1899-1989	Sect C
Simon	Cathleen Estep	May 17, 1958 - Aug 11, 1997	Sect D
Sims	James Russell, Sr.	PVT US Army, Oct 31, 1944 - Feb 28, 1991	Sect B
Sims	Shirley J.	May 8, 1939 - Blank	Sect B
Sims	William L.	Dec 25, 1941 - Sep 5, 1989	Sect B
Sims	William L.	SGT US Army Vietnam, Dec 25, 1941 - Sep 5, 1989	Sect B
Sizemore	Dale Linn	Infant Son Jun 1, 1975	Sect A
Sizemore	Darrell Linn	Oct 11, 1955 - Blank	Sect A
Sizemore	Dawnya Lynn	Jun 3, 1978 - Dec 3, 1991	Sect A
Sizemore	Lincoln	Feb 18, 1931 - Nov 15, 1998	Sect A
Sizemore	Rosemary	Dec 5, 1956 - Blank	Sect A
Sizemore	Shirley Adkins	Dec 17, 1936 - Blank	Sect A

Calvary Cemetery Old and New Sections

Surname	Given Name	Details	Section
Skeene	Clarence E.	Oct 19, 1925-Sep 3, 1987, Jun 14, 1947 wed Pauline C. Coffey	Sect C
Skeene	Clarence Edward	CPL US Marine Corps WWII, Oct 19, 1925 - Sep 3, 1987	Sect C
Skeene	David Joseph	May 12, 1956 - Aug 16, 2000	Sect C
Skeene	James H.	US Army Vietnam, Apr 22, 1948 - Oct 3, 1997	Sect C
Skeene	James H.	Apr 22, 1948 - Oct 3, 1997	Sect C
Skeene	Jeremy J.	Oct 23, 1975 - Apr 28, 2008	Sect C
Skeene	Pauline C. Coffey	Feb 20, 1927 - Blank, wed Jun 14, 1947 to Clarence E. Skeene	Sect C
Skeene	Steven Wesley	Feb 10, 1961 - Jan 12, 2009	Sect C
Skeene	William H.	1929-1990	Sect C
Skeene	William Harold	US Navy US Army, WWII, Korea, 1929-1990	Sect C
Smidley	Carrie A.	born Oct 10, 1892, died Jul 18, 1893	Sect B
Smidley	Emma C.	wife of William F. Smidley, born Jan 21, 1860, died Aug 24, 1942	Sect B
Smidley	William F.	born Apr 22, 1856, died Apr 14, 1898	Sect B
Smith	Albert J., Sr.	PVT US Army, Oct 25, 1925 - May 28, 2008	Sect A
Smith	Albert James, Sr.	Oct 25, 1925 - May 28, 2008	Sect A
Smith	Alex	1877-1964	Sect D
Smith	Anna Blanch	1911-1993	Sect D
Smith	Elizabeth Ann	wife of Richard Smith, 1920-1956	Sect D
Smith	Ernest E.	son of G & E Smith, died Sep 8, 1864, aged 3y 11m 15d	Old Section
Smith	Evelyn L.	Sep 4, 1929 to Nov 3, 2007, wed Jul 4, 1958 to Richard J. Smith	Sect B
Smith	illegible	of G & E Smith, born May 4, 1866, died Jun 23, 1874	Old Section
Smith	Infant Dau	of G & E Smith, died Apr 20, 1865, aged 1m 21d	Old Section
Smith	Infant Daughter	Nov 3, 1940 dau of Robert and Blanch Smith	Sect D
Smith	Larry Eithel	May 15, 1957 -Apr 15, 1978, husband of Branda, son of Eithel and Bernice Smith	Sect C
Smith	Lucy B.	wife of Peter C. Smith, Sep 15, 1841 - Jul 8, 1908	Sect D
Smith	Mary Lucille	Mar 31, 1912 - Dec 8, 1990	Sect B
Smith	Maurice Edwin	son of Robert and Blanch Smith, Dec 18, 1932 - Jan 29, 1933	Sect D
Smith	Nathan	Feb 10, 1908 - Blank	Sect B
Smith	Peter C.	May 7, 1837 - Sep 23, 1915	Sect D
Smith	Polly	1879-1937	Sect D
Smith	Richard J.	Apr 21, 1918 - Dec 16, 1996, wed Jul 4, 1958 to Evelyn L.	Sect B
Smith	Robert Roy	1903-1994	Sect D
Smith	Rosetta M.	dau of G & E Smith, born 17th 1874, died 26th, 1874	Old Section
Smyzer	David H.	son of AH and JF Smyzer, died Mar 21, 1883, aged 2y 3m 11d	Old Section
Smyzer	infants	daughters of AH & JF Smyzer	Old Section
Snider	Carroll A.	Ohio PFC SVC Co. 31, Infantry WWII, BSM, Feb 25, 1921 - Mar 24, 1959	Sect D
Snider	Carroll A.	1921-1959	Sect D
Snider	Catherine	botn Oct 8, 1791, died Jun 28, 1878	Old Section

Calvary Cemetery Old and New Sections

Surname	Given Name	Details	Section
Snider	Daisy M.	1911-1987	Sect D
Snider	John J.	1901-1968	Sect D
Snider	John J.	born Mar 27, 1819, died Apr 7, 1894	Old Section
Snider	Lavella L.	1911-1990	Sect D
Snider	Lois M.	Aug 5, 1930 - Mar 14, 1992	Sect C
Snider	Marsha L.	Feb 15, 1960 - Jun 13, 1997	Sect A
Snider	Minerva	born Nov 23, 1817 - no death date	Old Section
Snider	William	born Apr 1, 1794, died May 22, 1871	Old Section
Sowers	Jessie Dean	Mar 19, 1980 - Oct 10, 1980	Sect A
Steinle	Albert	1878-1937	Sect B
Steinle	Anna M.	1871-1959	Sect D
Steinle	Caroline	(mother) 1837-1929	Sect B
Stephens	Etna F.	1878-1964	Old Section
Stephenson	Florence	died Jun 12, 1854, aged 77y 5m 15d	Old Section
Stephenson	Lemuel	died Oct 9, 1837, aged 66y 3m	Old Section
Stevens	Elizabeth P.	dau of Thomas and Harriet Stevens, died Jul 29, 1872, aged 31y 10m.21d	Old Section
Stevens	Harriet Hines	wife of Thomas W. Stevens, 1807-1899	Old Section
Stevens	John	son of Thomas and Harriett Stevens, 1842-1906	Old Section
Stevens	Josie Baum	wife of MC Stevens, born Apr 25, 1847, died Jun 30, 1879	Old Section
Stevens	Laura B.	1850-1916	Sect D
Stevens	Margaret	1866-1937	Sect D
Stevens	Mark C.	1838-1915	Sect D
Stevens	Nelson H.	born Nov 17, 1836, died Jan 19, 1888	Old Section
Stevens	Thomas	1884-1915	Sect D
Stevens	Thomas W.	born at Acworth, N.H., born May 29, 1806, died Jul 23, 1878	Old Section
Stewart	Alonzo H.	son of TC and Eliza J. Stewart, died Jun 5, 1850, aged 1y 14d	Old Section
Stewart	George	died Nov 3, 1873 in 24th year	Old Section
Stewart	John D.	died May 4, 1854, aged 38 years	Old Section
Stewart	Sharon Lee	Apr 18, 1955 - Oct 20, 1996	Sect A
Stewart	William J.	son of William and Sarah Stewart, died Jun 13, 1850 in 26th year	Old Section
Stillwell	James H.	1925-2003	Sect A
Stone	Eva Lee	1927-1998	Sect C
Stone	Robert E.	SGT US Army WWII, Nov 13, 1920 - Jan 19, 1983	Sect C
Stone	Robert E.	1920-1983	Sect C
Stree	Henry	born May 25, 1823, died Feb 8, 1897	Sect D
Sturgill	Charles E.	Nov 4, 1933 - Sep 10, 2009, wed Aug 2, 1958 to Josephine Eversole	Sect C
Sturgill	Edna	Jun 17, 1903 - Jul 3, 1994	Sect C
Sturgill	G. Robert	PVT US Army WW1, Sep 12, 1892 - Dec 2, 1982	Sect C

37

Calvary Cemetery Old and New Sections

Sturgill	Josephine Eversole	May 25, 1942 - Blank, wed Aug 2, 1958 to Charles E. Sturgill	Sect C
Sturgill	Otis D.	Mar 18, 1930 - Sep 14, 1981	Sect C
Sturgill	Peggy L.	Mar 23, 1934 - Blank	Sect C
Sturgill	Robert	Sep 12, 1892 - Dec 2, 1982	Sect C
Swope	Bertha	dau of BT & MA Swope, July 29, 1880 - Oct 31, 1882	Old Section
Swope	Byron T.	born Sep 27, 1853, died Jan 10, 1889	Old Section
Swope	John S.	born Jan 27, 1827, died Apr 2, 1894	Old Section
Swope	Johnnie	born Jun 30, 1889, died Jun 21, 1891	Sect B
Swope	Mary A.	wife of NR Swope, born Jun 20, 1832, died Jun 19, 1889, 56y 11m 29ds	Old Section
Swope	Mary J.	dau of John and Sarah Swope, died Apr 19, 1865, 8 m 23d	Old Section
Swope	Nelson R.	1828-1899	Old Section
Swope	Sarah A. E. M. Thompson	wife of JS Swope, born Apr 11, 1825, died Mar 1, 1885	Old Section
Swope	Sarah Louella	born Jun 2, 1866, died Oct 24, 1871	Old Section
Swope	W. J., MD	born Sep 5, 1856, died Dec 2, 1887	Old Section
Sword	Jerry C.	1889-1973	Sect D
Tatman	Mary	wife of Joseph Tatman, died Dec 19, 1848, aged 34y 10m 27d	Old Section
Taulbee	Boyd	Aug 7, 1932 - Dec 31, 1997, wed Jul 2, 1955 to Leona Rose Boots	Sect C
Taulbee	Leona Rose Boots	Sep 4, 1937 - Feb 10, 2011, wed Jul 2, 1955 to Boyd Taulbee	Sect C
Taylor	Aquila	born Aug 7, 1762, died Oct 4, 1849, 77y 1m 29ds	Old Section
Taylor	Mary A.	dau of Aquilla and Rachel Taylor, died May 1, 1844 in 34th year	Old Section
Taylor	Rachel	wife of A. Taylor, died Feb 13, 1845 - 73 years	Old Section
Taylor	Steven A.	Jun 7, 1989 - Jun 1, 2007	Sect B
Terry	Flossie	Nov 30, 1912 - Apr 23, 1977	Sect C
Terry	Ted Roy	Mar 9, 1913 - Sep 1, 1974	Sect C
Terry	Terri	no dates	Sect C
Terwillegar	Jane	dau of Abraham and Permelia Terwillegar, born Jun 8, 1844, died Jul 11, 1844	Old Section
Terwilliger	Eliza	consort of Harvey Terwilliger, died Aug 16, 1841, aged 32y 10m 10d	Old Section
Thomas	Helen C.	1921-1995	Sect B
Thomas	Henry D.	Jun 26, 1929 - Jul 11, 2003	Sect B
Thomas	Shirlie	S1 US Navy WWII, 1911-1979	Sect B
Thompson	A.S.B.	died Oct 27, 1857, aged 64y 11m 14d	Old Section
Thompson	Berzelus Bosconi	son of R & Rev Wm Thompson, died Dec 14, 1837 60 d	Old Section
Thompson	David H. Colglazer	son of John & Sarah Thompson, died Feb 3, 1835 in 23rd year	Old Section
Thompson	Elizabeth	wife of ASB Thompson, died Nov 15, 1857, aged 58y 9m 11d	Old Section
Thompson	Elizabeth	wife of Rev William J. Thompson, died Jul 22, 1854, aged 67y 2m 15d	Old Section
Thompson	George W.	born Aug 8, 1835, died Dec 23, 1912	Sect B
Thompson	John	born Feb 22, 1789, died Jan 16, 1835	Old Section

Calvary Cemetery Old and New Sections

Surname	Given Name	Notes	Section
Thompson	Lewis Garrett	son of John & Sarah Thompson, died Feb 4, 1835 in 6th year	Old Section
Thompson	Lucretia	consort of Rev Wm J. Thompson, died Jun 17, 1835 in 65th year	Old Section
Thompson	Martha J.	May 22, 1840 - May 19, 1922	Sect B
Thompson	Rachel A.L.	dau of Berry & Elizabeth Thompson, died Sep 25, 1835, aged 3y 1m 6d	Old Section
Thompson	Rebecca	dau of William J and Lucretia Thompson, born Nov 19, 1798, died Jul 18, 1832	Old Section
Thompson	Rebecca	dau of John and Sarah Thompson, died Oct 23, 1830 in 17th yr.	Old Section
Thompson	Richard W.	son of AS & E Thompson, died Oct 9, 1838, aged 7y 9m	Old Section
Thompson	Ruhamah	2nd consort of Rev Wm J. Thompson, died Nov 29, 1837 in her 33rd year	Old Section
Thompson	Sarah	wife of John Thompson, died Jan 26, 1835 in 45th year	Old Section
Thompson	W. L., Dr.	died Aug 18, 1850, aged 30y 11m 3d	Old Section
Thompson	William J., Jr.	died Sep 15, 1845 - 24y 1m	Old Section
Thompson	William J., Rev	born Nov 2, 1767, died Jan 3, 1862, aged 94y 2m 1d	Old Section
Thompson	Wilson Lee	son of J & S Thompson, died Feb 3, 1835 in her 13th year hard to read)	Old Section
Tomlinson	Shelia	Oct 26, 1951 - Oct 13, 1979	Sect A
Tompkins	Florence Belle	dau of NW & NH Tompkins, died Jan 10, 1864, aged 11y 9m 9d	Old Section
Tompkins	Laura Jane	dau of NW & NH Tompkins, died Oct 8, 1863, aged 5y 8m 2d	Old Section
Tompkins	Lida May	dau of NU and N Tompkins, born Nov 22, 1865, died Nov 27, 1890	Sect A
Tompkins	Nackey H.	wife of NU Tompkins, born Feb 17, 1822, died Jan 15, 1902, aged 79y 10m 28ds	Sect A
Tompkins	Nicholas W.	died Dec 10, 1867, aged 49y 4m 5d	Old Section
Trees	Benjamin F.	Father 1842-1921	Old Section
Trees	Elizabeth Stevens	1869-1950	Old Section
Trees	J.P.	1876-1876	Old Section
Trees	Laura	Mother 1843-1906	Old Section
Trees	W. E.	1868-1924	Old Section
Tucker	Dorcas	wife of N. Tucker, died May 21, 1837, 29 years	Sect B
Tucker	John C.	son of N & D Tucker, died Sep 21, 1837, aged 6m 25ds	Old Section
Turner	Clementine	1865-1952	Sect B
Turner	J. M., Rev	1873-1935	Sect B
Turner	James A. or Thomas A.	son of JH & RG Turner, died Nov 21, 1861, aged 2m 22d	Old Section
Turner	Rachel G.	wife of Joseph H. Turner, died Jan 16, 1863, aged 23y 7m 16d	Old Section
Turner	Rachel H.	dau of JH & RG Turner, died Mar 26, 1863, aged 3m 1d	Old Section
Turpin	Peterfield	born Jul 18, 1812, died Dec 5, 1839	Old Section
Turton	Anna	1874-1919	Sect A
Turton	Chase	1870-1896	Sect A
Turton	infant	1894	Sect A
Turton	Ralph E.	1895-1968	Sect A
Udry	Anne Mae	Jul 4, 1917 - Jun 24, 1992	Sect B

Calvary Cemetery Old and New Sections

Surname	Given name	Details	Section
Uhlenbrock	Carrie Benjamine	born Apr 1, 1875, died May 14, 1914	Sect B
Uhlenbrock	John	born Sep 6, 1804, died Mar 17, 1896	Sect B
Uhlenbrock	John T.	born Oct 23, 1845, died Jan 20, 1896	Sect B
Uhlenbrock	Louise	born Mar 29, 1849, died Aug 30, 1879	Old Section
Uhlenbrock	Wilhelmina Adriann	born Nov 12, 1851, died Nov 10, 1908	Sect B
unknown	Mother and Sister	right by John Schwab Family monument	Sect D
unknown		by Joyce Caudill	Sect B
unknown		next to Joshua Poe	Sect A
Utter	Amanda	consort of WB Utter, died Apr 12, 1841, aged 26years	Old Section
Utter	Archie	1880-1924	Sect B
Utter	Carrie	1880-1958	Sect B
Utter	Ellizan	infant dau of Amanda and WB Utter, died Aug 21, 1840, aged 4m	Old Section
Utter	Georgia Elberg	PFC US Marine Corps, WWII, Aug 12, 1923 - Oct 8, 1985	Sect B
Utter	Joseph William	SSGT US Army, Air Corps, WWII, Jun 22, 1920 - Mar 3, 1995	Sect B
Vaughan	Beverly	Recent no info	Sect A
Vaughan	Gertrude R.	Dec 22, 1927 - Jan 10, 1996	Sect A
Vaughan	Minnie R.	1892-1961	Sect A
Vaughan	Robert O.	SGT US Army WWII, Bronze Start Medal - Purple Heart. 83rd and 104th WWII., Jul 17, 1924 - Oct 7, 2009	Sect C
Vaughan	Robert O.	Jul 17, 1924 - Oct 7, 2009, wed Feb 9, 1946 to Ruth Ora Cohen	Sect C
Vaughan	Robert Walter	AR US Navy Vietnam, Nov 2, 1946 - Sep 16, 2008	Sect C
Vaughan	Ruth Ora Cohen	Aug 6, 1924 - Mar 24, 1999	Sect C
Vaughan	Virgil R.	Sgt US Army WWII, Jun 6, 1918 - Oct 9, 1998	Sect A
Vaughan	Virgil R.	US Marine Corps, Jun 15, 1887 - Apr 13, 1968	Sect A
Vaughan	Virgil R., Jr.	Jun 6, 1918 - Oct 9, 1998	Sect A
Vaughn	Virgil R., Sr.	1887-1968	Sect A
Vogt	Jason Richard	Nov 8, 1984 - Oct 11, 2002	Sect D
Wade	William	1844-1918	Sect A
Walls	Felisha A.	Nov 11, 1972 - Jan 30, 2000	Sect B
Warden	Carl E.	Indiana Tec5 999 Engr TDWY Brg Co. WWII, Jul 3, 1916 - Jul 25, 1966	Sect D
Warden	Charles T.	1909-1942	Sect D
Warden	Helen E.	Jun 27, 1937 - Jul 9, 1996	Sect D
Warden	James R.	Aug 5, 1933 - Feb 28, 2011	Sect D
Warden	James Robert	SP3 US Army, Korea, Aug 5, 1933 - Feb 28, 2011	Sect D
Warden	James W.	1914-1980	Sect D
Warden	Mary L.	1878-1952	Sect D
Warden	Mary L.	1914-1998	Sect D

Calvary Cemetery Old and New Sections

Surname	Given Name	Details	Section
Warden	Ruth A.	1910-2001	Sect D
Warden	William M.	1877-1955	Sect D
Ware	Larry D.	1950 - Blank	Sect D
Ware	Nancy L.	1950-1969	Sect D
Ware	Ressie S.	US Army, WWII, Feb 14, 1912 - Dec 7, 1990	Sect D
Ware	Ressie S.	Feb 14, 1912 - Dec 7, 1990	Sect D
Ware	Vera K.	Jun 12, 1924 - Dec 1, 2006	Sect D
Watson	Ada E.	wife of JL Watson, born Oct 27, 1846, died Sep 24, 1880	Old Section
Watson	Dana E.	SP5 US Army, May 9, 1951 - Apr 25, 2008	Sect A
Watson	Delores M.	1920-2003	Sect A
Watson	J. L.	born Dec 22, 1838, died Mar 28, 1916	Old Section
Watson	K. V.	Jul 26, 1876 - Jun 1, 1924	Old Section
Watson	Kevan Lee	PV2 US Army, Jul 22, 1961 - Aug 31, 1985	Sect A
Watson	Kevan Lee	Jul 22, 1961 - Aug 31, 1985	Sect A
Watson	Warren	son of JL & AE Watson, born Oct 25, 1872, died Nov 23, 1873	Old Section
Watson	William E.	1917-1983	Sect A
Watson	William Edward	Maj US Army, WWII, Sep 18, 1917 - May 9, 1983	Sect A
Wear	Betty L.	Dec 24, 1932 - Apr 12, 2010	Sect B
Wear	Junior L.	Apr 25, 1928 - Blank	Sect B
Wedding	Ann Richards	wife of John Wedding, born Oct 29, 1796, died Dec 17, 1880	Old Section
Wedding	Margaret E.	dau of James W. & Sarah Wedding, died Aug 9, 1860, aged 3m 9d	Old Section
Wedding	Mary M.	wife of John Wedding, died May 25, 1858, aged 70y 3m 15d	Old Section
Wedding	Sarah J.	wife of James W. Wedding, died Sep 12, 1860, aged 21y 6m 9d	Old Section
Weding	John	died Mar 17, 1864, aged 81y 8m 18d	Old Section
Weimer	Audrey Utter	1907-1935	Sect B
Welch	Anna	wife of Darius Welch, born Jul 16, 1855, died Jan 9, 1877	Old Section
Wells	Emma L.	Feb 24, 1918 - Blank, wed Dec 23, 1939 to William P. Wells	Sect C
Wells	William P.	Oct 31, 1915 - Dec 3, 1999, wed Dec 23, 1939 to Emma L.	Sect C
Wells	William Palmer	PO2 US Navy WWII, Oct 31, 1915 - Dec 3, 1999	Sect C
Welsh	Albert	born Jun 20, 1821, died Dec 31, 1893	Old Section
Welsh	Andrew B.	son of DR and Jane Welsh, died Aug 29, 1853, aged 21y 8m	Old Section
Welsh	George P.	son of A & J Welsh, died Apr 9, 1881, aged 23y 7m 3d	Old Section
Welsh	Jane	wife of A. Welsh, died Apr 15, 1882, aged 56y 10m 11d	Old Section
White	Gerald P.	Nov 24, 1956 - Jun 24, 1999	Sect D
White	Gerald Paul	PVT US Army, Nov 24, 1956 - Jun 24, 1996	Sect D
White	John M.	Jun 24, 1919 - Oct 9, 1977	Sect D
White	John Matthew	PFC US Marine Corps, WWII, 1919-1977	Sect D
Wiggins	Ada Friend	Jan 27, 1879 - Feb 9, 1950	Sect D

Calvary Cemetery Old and New Sections

Surname	Given Name	Details	Section
Wiley	Amy J.	wife of JR Wiley, died Oct 13, 1877, aged 33y 7m 3d	Old Section
Wiley	Elizabeth	wife of JR Wiley, born Mar 6, 1842, died Sep 1, 1914	Old Section
Wiley	J. R.	1842-1904	Old Section
Wiley	Maggie E.	died Feb 22, 1852, aged 6y 4m	Old Section
Wiley	Mary Richards	wife of SP Wiley, born Jun 30, 1818, died May 21, 1891	Old Section
Wiley	Othe K.	died Feb 17, 1852, aged 4y 4m	Old Section
Wiley	Sammie	died Apr 1, 1852, aged 1y 5m 11d	Old Section
Wiley	Samuel P.	died Jul 17, 1876, aged 68y 4m 7d	Old Section
Wiley	Samuel W.	son of JR and AL Wiley, 1874-1898	Old Section
Wifert	Bertha E.	Sep 27, 1903 - Dec 8, 1978	Sect D
Wifert	Mollie	1877-1949	Sect D
Wifert	William F.	1867-1934	Sect D
Williams	Carl C.	May 15, 1909 - May 7, 1988, wed May 20, 1933 to Mattie S.	Sect B
Williams	Mattie S.	Dec 24, 1908 - Feb 19, 2004, wed May 20, 1933 to Carl C. Williams	Sect B
Willis	William A.	son of John and Patience Willis, died Nov 14, 1843, aged 3y 4m	Old Section
Wilson	Ida T.	1878-1928	Sect D
Wilson	Lela L.	1901-1947	Sect D
Wilson	Morton W.	1874-1963	Sect D
Wilson	Nancy	dec: Aug 20	Old Section
Wilson	Stanley	son of MW and Ida, May 30, 1915 - May 23, 1916	Sect D
Windsor	Charles III	1979-2004	Sect D
Windsor	Charles W. IV	2000 -2001	Sect D
Windsor	Charlie W. II	Apr 13, 1979 - Mar 17, 2004	Sect D
Winston	Vevia	1907-1993	Sect A
Winston	Wilbur J.	1908-1967	Sect A
Winters	Edward Lee	US Army, Sep 30, 1938 - Feb 22, 2001	Sect D
Wolf	Andrea Ellan	Jan 8, 1987 - Jan 16, 1987	Sect D
Wolf	Hazel S.	Oct 5, 1902 - Feb 7, 1989	Sect B
Wolf	James E.	Aug 24, 1937 - Aug 27, 1997	Sect D
Wolf	Joseph E.	Ohio PVT 136 Field Arty 37 Div. Apr 25, 1898 - Sep 24, 1945	Sect B
Wolf	Joshua James	Dec 21, 1983 - Nov 27, 2005	Sect A
Wood	B. G.	born Nov 16, 1848, died Jan 6, 1904	Sect B
Wood	David	1815-1846	Sect B
Wood	Dowty Lee	1852-1884	Old Section
Wood	Howard E.	son of BG & LF Wood, Feb 17, 1881 - Nov 17, 1889	Sect B
Wood	Jane	died Mar 28, 1855	Old Section
Wood	Joseph H.	son of BG & LF Wood, Jan 5, 1894 - Jan 1, 1896	Sect B
Wood	Laura B. Abrams	wife of WH Wood, born Nov 10, 1851, died Dec 15, 1894, aged 42y 10m 5ds	Sect B

Calvary Cemetery Old and New Sections

Surname	Given Name	Details	Section
Wood	Leannah	wife of Harvey Wood, 1827-1899	Sect B
Wood	Lydia F. McGohan	wife of B. G. Wood, born Aug 2, 1853, died Dec 4, 1900	Sect B
Wood	Mary Day	wife of David Wood, 1821-1906	Sect B
Wood	W. Guy	son of BG & LF Wood, Jul 2, 1883 - Nov 18, 1889	Sect B
Wood	W. Harvey	1817-1878	Old Section
Wrigglesworth	Alice C.	1896-1915, dau of Carl and Dora Wrigglesworth	Sect D
Wrigglesworth	Carr	1860-1933	Sect D
Wrigglesworth	Dora D.	1873-1944	Sect D
Wrigglesworth	John	May 5, 1870 - May 14, 1961	Sect D
Wrigglesworth	Minnie	wife of John Wrigglesworth, Aug 5, 1871 - Mar 6, 1907	Sect D
Wrigglesworth	Rachel	wife of William H. Wrigglesworth. Aug 9, 1837 - Jun 22, 1907	Sect D
Wrigglesworth	William H.	Jul 13, 1836 - Apr 14, 1907	Sect D
Wyatt	Bessie H.	1910-1986	Sect B
Wyatt	Beve J.	1914-1997	Sect B
Wyatt	Harriett	wife of Jonathan Wyatt, died May 23, 1884, aged 73y 6m 12d	Old Section
Wyatt	Jane	our mother, died Dec 17, 1870, aged 73y 5m 17d	Old Section
Wylie	Candace Renee	Aug 22, 1982, 3 m 18d	Sect A
Young	Audrey J.	Jan 27, 1964 - Nov 20, 2004, mother of J. J.	Sect C
Young	Clayton Russ	Apr 21, 1959 - Aug 29, 2009	Sect C
Young	Sherry	Mar 13, 1962 - Feb 22, 2004, separate cross marker states Feb 2, 2004	Sect C
Youngman	Bessie L.	1887-1889	Sect B
Youngman	Mildred	1856-1928	Sect B
Youngman	Robert F.	1848-1922	Sect B
Youngman	Sallie F.	1884-1886	Sect B
Youngman	Wallace R.	1874-1888	Sect B
Youtsey	Randall Gene	SRA US Air Force, SGT US Marine Corps, Apr 28, 1957 - Apr 21, 2006	Sect A